CLASSIC SERMONS

ON

WORSHIP

Compiled by

Warren W. Wiersbe

KREGEL PUBLICATIONS
Grand Rapids, Michigan 49501

Classic Sermons on Worship, compiled by Warren W. Wiersbe. © 1988 by Kregel Publications, a division of Kregel, Inc., P. O. Box 2607, Grand Rapids, MI 49501. All rights reserved.

Library of Congress Cataloging-in-Publication Data

Classic Sermons on Worship, compiled
by Warren W. Wiersbe. (Kregel classic sermons series)
  Includes index.

  1. Worship—Sermons. 2. Sermons, American. 3. Sermons, English. I. Wiersbe, Warren W. II. Series: Kregel classic sermons series.

BV10.2C53   1988   248.3   87-29721

  ISBN   0-8254-4037-8 (pbk.)

2 3 4 5 Printing/Year 92 91 90 89

Printed in the United States of America

CLASSIC SERMONS

ON

WORSHIP

KREGEL CLASSIC SERMONS SERIES

Dedicated with grateful appreciation to two of my boyhood pastors

REV. EVERETT A. OSTROM

and

DR. WILLIAM TAYLOR

Your ministry to me, your prayers on my behalf, your life-long friendship, and your example of service, have been a source of encouragement and blessing.

Thank you!

CONTENTS

PREFACE

THE *CLASSIC SERMONS SERIES* is an attempt to assemble
and publish meaningful sermons from master preachers
about significant themes.

These are *sermons*, not essays or chapters taken from
books about themes. Not all of these sermons could be
called "great," but all of them are *meaningful*. They
apply the truths of the Bible to the needs of the human
heart, which is something that all effective preaching
must do.

While some are better known than others, all of the
preachers, whose sermons I have selected, had important ministries and were highly respected in their day.
The fact that a sermon is included in this volume does
not mean that either the compiler or the publisher
agrees with or endorses everything that the man did,
preached, or wrote. The sermon is here, because it has a
valued contribution to make.

These are sermons about *significant* themes. The
pulpit is no place to play with trivia. The preacher has
thirty minutes in which to help mend broken hearts,
change defeated lives, and save lost souls; and he can
never accomplish this demanding ministry by distribut-
ing homiletical tid-bits. In these difficult days, we do not
need "clever" pulpiteers who discuss the times; we need
dedicated ambassadors who will preach the eternities.

The reading of these sermons can enrich your own
spiritual life. The studying of them can enrich your own
skills as an interpreter and expounder of God's truth.
However God uses these sermons in your own life and
ministry, my prayer is that His Church around the world
will be encouraged and strengthened.

Back to the Bible Broadcast   WARREN W. WIERSBE
Lincoln, Nebraska

Worship

John A. Broadus (1827-1895) has long been
recognized as the "Dean of American teachers of
homiletics." His work *The Preparation and Delivery of
Sermons*, in its many revisions, has been a basic
textbook for preachers since it was first published in
1870. Born and educated in Virginia, Broadus pastored
the Baptist church at Charlottesville, and in 1859
became Professor of New Testament Interpretation and
of Homiletics at the Southern Baptist Theological
Seminary. He was named president of the school in
1888. The sermon "Worship" was preached at the
dedication of the Second Baptist Church of St. Louis in
1879, and was taken from *Sermons and Addresses* by
John A. Broadus, published by Hodder and Stoughton
in 1886.

1

Worship

God is a Spirit, and they that worship him must worship him in spirit and in truth (John 4:24).

JESUS WAS TIRED. The little that we know of the history just before, enables us to see why He should have been tired.

He had been, for long months, engaged in active efforts to save men's souls—to lift men out of their sluggishness and worldliness toward God. That is hard work for mind and heart. And He had been at work among many who were hostile. Some of the disciples of John were envious that their master was decreasing and another was increasing, though John said it was right and good; and when the Pharisees heard that Jesus was now making and baptizing more disciples than John, they were jealous. They made it needful that He should withdraw from Judea, as so often during His brief ministry He had to withdraw from the jealously of His enemies or the fanaticism of His friends, and seek a new field. Worn out and perhaps sad at heart, the Redeemer sat alone by Jacob's well.

Our artists owe us yet two companion pictures: the one of Jesus, as the disciples saw Him when they turned back to look, on their way to buy food, as He sat and rested, leaning with limbs relaxed, with face weary, yet gentle; and the other of Jesus as they found Him when they came back, sitting up now with an animated look on His face, busily, eagerly talking.

Ah! there was an opening to do good, and He who "went about doing good" would give up even his needed rest, and often did, we know, to do good to the least and the lowest. The disciples wondered not that He was ready to do good; they had seen that often before. But they wondered that He was talking with a woman, for that was contrary to the dignity of a man according to

the ideas of that time and country,—to be seen talking
with a woman in public. They wondered; they knew not
yet what manner of spirit they were of,—that they had to
deal with high saving truths that break through all
weak conventionalities.

They would have wondered more if they had known
what He knew full well—that it was a woman of bad
character; and yet He saw in her potential for good, and
He did win her that day to faith in the Messiah who had
come, and He sent her forth to tell others to come and see
"a man who had told her all things whatsoever she did."

But she shrank in the process. Beautiful and wonderful it is to see how admirably our Lord led the casual
conversation with a stranger so as to introduce the pro-
foundest spiritual truths.

My Christian friends, let me not fail to point your
attention to this. I know no art of social life more needful
to be cultivated in our time and country than the art of
skillfully introducing religion into general conversation. It is a difficult task. It requires tact and skill to do
this in such a way as to accomplish much good and no
harm; but it is worth all your efforts. Old and young,
men and women, yea—shall I say it?—especially young
ladies, who are Christians, with that control which
young ladies have in our American society, need to cultivate few things so much as just that power which the
Savior here showed. Oh! beautiful, blessed example of
Jesus! How it shines more and more as we study and
strive to imitate it! And not only did He lead on toward
religious truth, but He knew how, in a quiet, skillful
way, to awaken her consciousness to a realization of her
sinfulness, so that she might come near to spiritual
truth. She shrank from it, I said, as people will often
shrink from us when we try to bring truth home to their
souls. She shrank, and while not wishing to turn the
conversation entirely away from religious things, she
would turn it away to something not so uncomfortably
close, and so she asked Him about a great question much
discussed.

"Sir, I perceive that thou art a prophet. Our fathers did

worship in this mountain," and right up the steep slopes of Mount Gerizim she would point to the mount high above them, where were the ruins of the old temple of the Samaritans, destroyed a century and a half before. "Our fathers worshiped in this mountain; and ye say that in Jerusalem is the place where men ought to worship. O prophet, which is it?" Again the Redeemer, while He answers her question, will turn it away from all matters of form and outward service, and strike deep by a blow into the spiritual heart of things. "Woman, believe me, the hour is coming, when neither in this mountain nor in Jerusalem shall ye worship the Father." He will not fail to imply in passing that Jerusalem had been the right place. "Ye worship that which ye know not. We worship that which we know, for salvation is from the Jews"–he only mentions that in passing–"but the hour cometh and now is, when the true worshipers shall worship the Father in spirit and truth, for such doth the Father seek to be his worshipers."

Only spiritual worship will be acceptable to God; this is what He seeks, and, more than that, this is what the very nature of the case requires. "For God is a Spirit, and they that worship Him must worship Him in spirit and in truth."

I wish to speak of the worship of God, and I shall ask two very simple questions about it, and try briefly to answer each of them.

Why should we worship God? How should we worship God?

Why Should We Worship God?

A man might well draw back and fear to say one word as to reasons why we should worship God. Oh! how high, and wide, and deep, is that theme! And yet it may be useful just to remind you of some things included in these expressions. Why ought we to worship God? Because it is due to Him; and because it is good for us.

1. That we should render to God worship is *due to Him.*

My dear friends, if we were but unconcerned spectators of *the glorious God and His wonderful works*, it ought to draw out our hearts to admiration and adoration and loving worship. The German philosopher, Kant, probably the greatest philosopher of modern times, said: "There are two things that always awaken in me, when I contemplate them, the sentiment of the sublime. They are the starry heavens and the moral nature of man." Oh! God made them both, and all there is of the sublime in either or in both is but a dim, poor reflection of the glory of Him who made them. Whatever there is in this world that is suited to lift up men's souls at all ought to lift them towards God.

Robert Hall said that the idea of God subordinates to itself all that is great, borrows splendor from all that is faith, and sits enthroned on the riches of the universe. More than that is true. I repeat, all that exalts our souls ought to lift them up toward God. Especially ought we to adore the holiness of God.

O sinful human beings, still you know that holiness is the crown of existence. There is not a human heart that does not somehow, sometimes love goodness. Find me the most wicked man in all your great city, and there are times when that man admires goodness. Yea, I imagine there are times when he hopes that somehow or other he may yet be good himself. When a man we love has died, we are prone to exaggerate in our funeral discourse, in our inscriptions on tombstones and the like—to exaggerate what? We seldom exaggerate much in speaking of a man's talents, or learning, or possessions, or influence, but we are always ready to exaggerate his goodness. We want to make the best of the man in that solemn hour. We feel that goodness is the great thing for a human being when he has gone out of our view into the world unseen.

And what is it that the Scriptures teach us is one of the great themes of the high worship of God, where worship is perfect? Long ago a prophet saw the Lord seated high on a throne in the temple, with flowing robes of majesty, and on either side adoring seraphs did bend and worship, and oh! what was it that was the theme of their worship? Was it God's power? Was it God's wisdom? You know what they said: "Holy, holy, holy, is the Lord of hosts. The whole earth is full of His glory." And there do come times, O my friends, to you and me, though we lift not holy hands, for we are sinful, though we dwell among a people of unclean lips, there come times to you and me when we want to adore the *holiness* of God.

And then think of His love and mercy! If you were only unconcerned spectators, I said, think of *His love and mercy!*

He hates sin. We know not how to hate sin as the holy God must hate it. And yet how He loves the sinner! How He yearns over the sinful! How He longs to save him! Oh, heaven and earth, God so loved the world that He gave His only begotten Son, that whosoever will have it so, might through Him be saved.

I know where that great provision, that mighty mercy is adored. I know from God's word that those high and glorious ones, who know far more than we do of the glorious attributes of the Creator and the wide wonders of His works, when they have sung their highest song of praise for God's character and for creation, will then strike a higher note as they sing the praises of redemption, for holiness and redemption are the great themes which the Scriptures make known to us of the worship in heaven. John saw in his vision how the four living creatures, representing the powers of nature, and the four and twenty elders, representing the saved of God, bowed in worship, and how a wide and encircling host of angels caught the sound, and how it spread wider still, till in all the universe it rolls, "salvation and honor and glory and power be unto Him that sitteth on the throne and unto the Lamb forever and ever (Rev. 5:13).

Holiness and redemption! We ought to adore if we had nothing to do with it, for we have a moral nature to appreciate it. And oh! are we unconcerned spectators? That most wonderful manifestation of God's mercy and love has been made toward us. And, if the angels find their highest theme of praise in what the gracious God

has done for us, how ought we to feel about it? Yea, there
is a sense in which, amid the infirmities of earth, we
can pay God a worship that the angels cannot themselves offer.

> Earth has a joy unknown in heaven;
> The new born bliss of sins forgiven.

And sinful beings here may strike, out of grateful
hearts for sins forgiven, a note of praise to God that shall
pierce through all the high anthems of the skies and
enter into the ear of the Lord God of Hosts.

2. But I said we ought to worship God, not only because
it is due to Him, but because *it is good for us.* Only the
worship of God can satisfy the highest and noblest aspirations of our natures.

When anything lifts us up, then we want God as the
climax of our exalted thought, and our thought itself is
imperfect without it. If you will look in the early morning light, upon the glory of the autumn woods, bright,
and so beautiful; if you gaze upon the splendor, as you
will do when this service is ended, of the nightly skies; if
you stand in awe before the great mountains, snow-clad
and towering, before Hermon, before the wonderful
mountains of our own wonderful West; if you go and gaze
in the silence of night upon the rush of your own imperial river, or stand by the seashore, and hear the mighty
waters rolling evermore, there swells in the breast something that wants God for its crown and for its completeness. There are aspirations in these strange natures of
ours that only God can satisfy. Our thinking is a mutilated fragment without God, and our hearts can never
rest unless they rest in God.

And *worship,* oh, *how it can soothe*! Yea, sometimes
worship alone can soothe our sorrows and our anxieties.
There come to all of us times when everything else does
fail us; there come times when we go to speak with
sorrowing friends and feel that all other themes are
weak and vain. You, wicked man yonder—you have gone
sometimes to visit a friend that was in great distress,

who had lost a dear child, it may be, or husband or wife; and as you have sat down by your friend and wanted to say something comforting, you have felt that everything else was vain but to point the poor sorrowing heart to God; and you felt ashamed of yourself that you did not dare to do that. How often have devout hearts found comfort in sorrow, found support in anxiety, by the worship of God; by the thought of submission to God and trust in God; a belief that God knows what He is doing; that God sees the end from the beginning; that God makes "all things work together for good to those that love him!"

And I add that *the worship of God nourishes the deepest root of morality* – individual and social. Morality cannot live upon mere ideas of expediency and utility. We have some philosophers in our day (and they show abilities and earnestness that command our respect, though they may seem to us to go so sadly and so far astray) who have persuaded themselves, alas! that Christianity must be flung aside; that belief in God even must be abandoned; but they are beginning to recognize the necessity for trying to tell the world what they are going to put in place of that, for the conservation of individual and social morality; and so they have told us that natural sympathy will lead us to recognize that we owe duties to others as well as ourselves. Natural sympathy is going to do that? Ah, I think not. Sometimes it will, if there is something mightier that can help. Often natural sympathy will fail. The root of morality is the sentiment of moral obligation.

What does it mean when your child begins to say, "I ought to do this" and "I ought not to do that?" What does it mean? "I ought." Some of the beasts around us are very intelligent. They seem to think in a crude fashion. They seem to reason in a rudimentary way. Our intellect is not peculiar to us. They have something of it but they show no sign of having the rudiments of the notion that "I ought" and "I ought not." It is the glory of man. It marks him in the image of the spiritual one that made him. And what is to nourish and keep alive and make strong that sentiment of moral obligation in our souls, unless it be the recognition of the fact that there is a God who gave us this high, moral, spiritual being; who made us for Himself; to whom we belong, because He made us, and because He made us to love Him until the sentiment of obligation to Him shall nourish in us the feeling of obligation to our fellow-men, who, like us, are made in His image.

But we are told that there is going to be a moral interregnum shortly; that so many cultivated people are rejecting all religion; that now there is danger that society will suffer until the new ideas can work themselves into popular favor. Yes, indeed, society would suffer but for one thing, and that is that still there are and still there will be not a few among the cultivated, and many, thank God! among those who are not blessed with cultivation, who hold fast their faith in the only true God and in Jesus Christ whom He has sent, and that will conserve society and hold up the very men who fancy they can do without Christianity.

For this reason, if there were no other, it would be worthwhile to build great and noble churches in our great cities, as we build monuments for other things to remind men of grand events and heroic deeds; so that if churches were never entered, they would be worth building as memorials, as reminders of God and eternity. Amid the homes of wealth and luxury, amid the splendid centers of commerce, and amid, alas! the palaces of vice, our churches stand serene and still, pointing up, like the Christian's hope, toward heaven. The thoughtless, the wayward, worldly and wicked will sometimes look as they pass, and as from the monuments over some heroic dead man, they catch a moment's impression for good, so from the church edifice itself they will catch a momentary impression of higher things, and be at least a little restrained from what is wrong and a little incited towards what is right.

And that is but the least of it. The great nourisher of morality in the individual and the community is not the mere outward symbol; it is the worship that is paid within. But I shall offer no more on this theme. How can a man tell the reasons why we should worship God? They are as high as heaven, as wide as the world, as vast as the universe; all existence and all conception—everything is a reason why we should worship God; and I turn to the other question, to which the text especially points.

How Should We Worship God?

I wish here to speak only of that line of thought which the text presents, How shall we worship God with spiritual worship?

The spiritual worship the text points out to us is essentially independent of localities. Time was when it was not so, when the best worship that was to be expected in the world depended upon holy places and impressive rites. In the childhood of the race these ideas were necessary, but Christianity came as the maturity of revealed religion, and declared that those ideas should prevail no longer; that true Christian spiritual worship is essentially independent of localities.

Dedicate a Place to Worship

My friends, under the Christian system you cannot make holy places; you cannot make a holy house. We speak very naturally and properly enough, if with due limitation, in the language of the Old Testament, about our places of worship, but we ought to remember constantly the limitations. You cannot consecrate a building in the light of Christianity. You can dedicate the building; you can *set it apart* to be used only for the worship of God; but you cannot make the house a holy house. It is an idea foreign to the intense spirituality which Jesus has taught us that belongs to the Christian idea of worship. Why, then, one might say, why should we have houses of worship? Not merely because if there is to be the worship of assemblies at all, with all the strange power that sympathy gives to aggregated worship, then there must be places of assembly. Rather because these soon become associated with the solemn worship we hold in them and sacred by their associations, and if we do not disturb those associations, if from the places where we hold solemn worship, we keep carefully away all that tends to violate those associations, they grow in power upon us. They do not make the place holy, but they make it easier by force of association and of beneficent habit for us to have holy thoughts and to pay holy worship in the place where we have often paid it before. So we can see why it is fit to set apart places of worship, houses of worship for God, though they be not in themselves holy, though spiritual worship is independent of locality.

Subordinates Worship All Externals

Let us rise to a broader view of the matter. Spiritual worship must subordinate all these externals.

Here I will offer a plain, unadorned, unimpassioned statement about this really practical matter, surely suitable to our circumstances, worthy to be discussed; for there are many extremes about it among men, and though you may not agree with my thought, it may help you to think the matter through for yourself. I offer, then, on the one hand, spiritual worship *must have* its externals. For while we are spiritual, like God, we are something else also. We have a material nature, and we are all closely linked and inter-dependent and acting upon each other continually. It is idle, then, to think that our worship will be all that it is capable of becoming if we try to keep it exclusively spiritual and give it no outward expression at all. When you try to pray in private by your own bedside, alone with your beating heart and your God, you are mistaken if you try to pray without couching your thought and feeling in words. We need the force of expression, though we utter not the words. We need to have the words in order to give clearness and form to our thought and our sentiment; and it is good even when alone, in low, solemn tones to speak out one's private prayer, for that seems somehow, by a law of our nature, to deepen the feeling which we thus outwardly express. And if we do so even in private prayer, how much more is it necessarily true in public worship!

We must have *expression* then for our worship, that there may be sympathy—expression that shall awaken and command sympathy. We must use the language of imagination and passion as used in the Scriptures. The Scriptures are full of the language of imagination and passion—language that is meant to stir the souls of men. And when we sing—sing in the simplest and plainest way, if you please—we are yet striving to use that as one of the externals of spiritual worship. We need it. We must have externals. Why, then—a man might ask, and men often have asked—why not have anything and everything that will contribute at all to help the expression and cherish the devout feeling? Why not have everything in architecture, everything in painting and statuary, everything in special garments, in solemn processions, in significant posture? Why not anything and everything that may at all help as an external expression of devout feeling? Let us consider this, I pray you. I said spiritual worship must have its externals, and now I repeat that it *must subordinate* those externals. Whatever externals it cannot subordinate it must discard, and the externals it does employ it must employ heedfully.

There are some things that awaken in some men a sort of fictitious, quasi-devout feeling, which you never would think of recommending as aids to devotion. Some persons when they use opium have a dreamy sort of devoutness, and some persons, even when they become drunk, show a morbid sort of religion. Yet who would think of saying that these are acts that aid devotion? But there are feelings that are right in themselves and noble in their place that do in some cases help to promote devotional feeling. The husband and wife, when they bow down with their children by their sides to pray together, and then, rising up, look lovingly into each other's eyes, find their devout feeling towards God heightened by their love for each other and their children. I can fancy that the young man and woman who both fear God and have learned to love each other may sometimes feel their devout sentiments truly heightened by this new, strange and beautiful affection which they have learned to feel for each other. That is so sometimes, and yet to recommend that as an avowed and systematic thing to be used as a help to devotion would be out of the question. Not everything, then, that may promote devotion is to be regularly used for this purpose.

Dangerous Aids to Worship

There are some things that look as if they were necessary and are very often recommended as helpful, and often employed as helps, that turn out to be dangerous and erroneous. Why can't we use pictures and statuary as helps to devotion? Why can't we employ them as proper means of making the thought of our Savior near and dear to us? Well, in all the ages of the world, the heathen have tried this. An educated young Hindoo, some years ago, educated in England, wrote an essay in which he complained bitterly that the Hindoos were accused of worshiping images, and quoted Cowper's beautiful poem entitled, "My Mother's Picture:"

> O, that those lips had language!
> Years have passed since thee I saw.

And he says, the picture of the poet's mother brought close and made real the thought of one long dead. That is the way, he said, that we use images. But that is not the way that the great mass of men use images in worship. They have often meant that at the outset; but how soon it degenerated and was degraded, and these things that were meant as helps to worship dragged down the aspirations of human hearts, instead of lifting them up! But, it seems to me, if I were to employ such helps in our time, persuading myself that they would be good, that I should feel it was wise to go back to the old ten commandments that we teach our children to repeat, and cut out the second commandment, that expressly forbids the use of graven images, because it necessarily leads to idolatry. I should cut that out. You can inquire, if you are curious to do so—and I say it in kindness—you can inquire whether those Christians in our own time who employ pictures and statues today as helps to devotion have mutilated the ten commandments. They were obliged to leave out that which their little children would say was forbidding what they do.

Aye, the world has tried that experiment widely and in every way, and it is found that though you might think that pictures and statuary would be helps to devotion, they turn out to be hurtful. They may help a few; they harm many.

Necessary Externals

But there are some of these things which we must have to some extent: church buildings, architecture, music, cultivated eloquence. How about these? We are obliged to have these. We must have the rude and coarse, if we have not the refined and elegant; and just what we may have in this respect depends, of course, upon what we have been accustomed to in our homes, our places of public assembly, our halls of justice. That which is natural, needful and good for some would utterly distract the attention of others.

Take a man from the most ignorant rural region, utterly unused to such things, and place him in this church next Sunday morning, and his attention would be utterly distracted by the architectural beauties of the place and the strange power of the music, and he would be scarcely able to have any other thought. These things would be hurtful to him; but to those who have been used to them and who, in their own churches, have been accustomed to elegance and beauty, or in the churches of others they sometimes enter, or in the great places of public assembly in the cities where they live, these things need not be hurtful to them. They may be helpful to them. Ah, my friends, they need to be used by us all with caution and with earnest efforts to make them helpful to devotion, or they will drag down our attention to themselves. Often it is so. You go home with your children, talking only about the beauty of your house of worship or the beauty of the music, and how soon your children will come to think and feel that that is all there is to come to church for, and how many there are who do thus think and feel.

It is easy to talk nonsense on the subject of *church music*. It is very difficult to talk wisely. But I think there is a distinction between secular and sacred music. I have seen places where they did not seem to know there was such a distinction. They seem to have obliterated it by using so much purely secular music in sacred worship. It is a distinction not easy to define, I know, but easy enough to comprehend on the part of one who is cultivated and has an ear for music and a heart for devotion. It is a distinction that ought always to be heedfully regarded. Our beautiful church music I delight in. I have sat here this afternoon and evening, and it has done me good to listen to it; but we must learn to use it as an aid to worship, or else we are using it wrong, and it will do us harm. We must not only cultivate the use and enjoyment of artistic music for the sake of enjoyment, but what is far more than enjoyment, we must cultivate the power of making it a help to religious worship. We must learn to do that, or we must refuse to have it.

We must learn to discard that which we cannot subordinate to spiritual worship, learn to use heedfully, with constant effort for ourselves and for our families and for our friends to use that which it is right to use, that it may help and not hinder. I pray you, then, do not go to asking people to come just to see your beautiful house of worship or to listen to your noble music. Some will come for that reason alone, and you cannot help it. But do not encourage such a thought. Talk about worship. Talk about these externals as helps to the solemn worship of God. Try to take that view of it. Try to make other people take that view of it. Be afraid for yourselves, and try to speak of it for its own sake and not for the sake of the aesthetic gratification it may give.

Real Spiritual Worship

And now, some closing words on worship, real spiritual worship. I think that in most of our churches—our churches that have no set ritual, no fixed form of worship—there is a disposition to underrate the importance of public worship; to think only of the preaching. I notice that in those churches, they always gave notice for preaching and not for worship, they only talk about the preacher and not the worship. They seem to think it makes little difference if they are too late for worship, provided they are there in time for the sermon. I notice that many preachers seem to give their whole thought to their sermon, and think nothing of preparing themselves for that high task, that solemn, responsible undertaking, to try to lift up the hearts of a great assembly in prayer to God. What I wish to say is, wherever that may be true, let us consider whether we ought not to take more interest in our worship, in the reading of God's Word for devotional impression, in solemn, sacred song and in humble prayer to God, in which we wish the hearts of the whole assembly to rise and melt together. It is true that we must have a care how we cultivate variety here, for the hearts of men seem to take delight in something of routine in their worship; they are rested if they know what comes next; they are harassed often if they are frequently disappointed and something quite unexpected comes in. We must keep our variety within limits, but within limits we must cultivate variety. I believe there should be more attention given to making our worship varied in its interest; and then, something far more important for the preacher and people is this.

We Must Put Heart Into Our Worship

We must not care merely to hear a man preach. I do not wish you to think less of preaching, but more of the other. We must put heart into our worship. Even the sermon is a two-sided thing—one side of it is part of our worship so far as it causes devotional feeling and lifts up the heart towards God, though on its other side of instruction and exhortation it is distinct from worship.

Now, I say, we must put heart in our worship. Do not venture to come to this beautiful place of worship, or whatever place of worship you attend, and just sit to see if the choir can stir you or to see if the preacher can stir you. Oh, stir up your own souls! It is your solemn duty when you go to engage with others in the worship of God—it is your duty to yourself, to others, to the pastor who wishes to lead your worship, to God, who wants the hearts of men, and who will have nothing but their hearts. I know how we feel. Worn by a week's toil, languid on the Lord's day through lack of our customary excitement, we go and take our places, jaded and dull, and we are tempted to think, "Now I will see whether the services can make any impression on me; whether the preacher can get hold of me—I hope they may," and we sit passive to wait and see. Oh, let us not dare thus to deal with the solemnity of the worship of God.

If we learn to worship aright, there will be beautiful and blessed consequences. It will bring far more of good to our own souls. It will make worship far more impressive to our children. Haven't you observed that it is getting to be one of the questions of our day how the Sunday school children are to be drawn to our public worship? We are often told that the preacher must try to make his sermon more attractive to children, and so he must. But let us also make our worship more impressive, and make our children feel that it is their duty to worship God, and try to bring them under the influence of this worship. I heard in Washington one of the foremost Sunday school laborers of this country, a Methodist minister, make this statement in private. He said: "Of late I have been telling the people everywhere, if your children cannot do both, cannot go to Sunday school and go to the public worship also, keep them away from the Sunday school, for they must go to the public worship." You may call that an extravagant statement. I am not sure that it is extravagant, but I am sure of this, that we need not merely try to make our preaching attract children, but try to make the worship so solemn, so real, so genuine, so earnest, that those strange little earnest hearts of our children will feel that there is something there that strikes to their souls.

And if you have true, fervent worship of God, the stranger that comes into your place of worship will feel it too. Have you not noticed when you go into some churches how quickly you perceive that you are in an atmosphere of hospitality and genuine kindness? There may be no parade, no speech-making. Yet in some places you may feel it, you feel it in the atmosphere, you feel it at once in your soul; you see a place where they are kindly and loving. So it ought to be, that when a man comes into your place of worship he shall very soon feel a something that pervades the atmosphere he breathes, from the look of the people, from the solemn stillness, from the unaffected earnestness he shall feel that these people are genuine, solemn worshipers of God. When he feels that, he will conclude that God is with you in truth, and there will be power to move his soul in your solemn worship.

May there be much of real spiritual worship in your church. When your hearts are full sometimes and you come and try to throw your souls into God's worship, may you be moved and melted; when you are sorely tempted sometimes and, coming to the house of God, try to lift your heart to Him in prayer, may you get good from the wise and loving words of the man you love to see stand before you as your pastor.

As your children grow up by your side and learn to delight with you in coming to the house of God in company, oh, may you be permitted to see more and more of them gladly coming to tell what great things God has done for their souls. And not only the children of your households, but strangers within your gates. May the stranger within your gates learn here to love your Savior and rejoice here to proclaim that love, and rise from the liquid grave to walk in newness of life.

And again and again, as you gather for that simplest of all ceremonies, as it is the most solemn, which Jesus

Himself appointed, in all simplicity taking bread and the cup in remembrance of Him, may He who sees men's hearts, see always that your hearts are towards Him in godly sincerity. And when offerings are asked here may they be offerings given as part of the worship of God, offerings that come from your hearts, offerings that are accepted by Him who wants the heart, offerings that are worthy of this beautiful home of your church life, and worthy to follow the gifts wherewith you have erected it. And time and again may there go forth those who have learned to worship here like successive swarms from fruitful hives to carry the same spirit of worship elsewhere, here and there, in great and growing and needy cities.

Yes, and when the young of your households begin to link those households more closely than ever together, and on the bridal day the brilliant procession comes sweeping up the aisle and all men's hearts are glad; may they always come reverently in the fear of the God they have here learned to worship. And you, when in the hour of your departure from the works of your hands, and from the worship that you have loved on earth, and slow and solemn up the aisle they bear the casket that holds all that is left to earth of you, and behind come sad-faced men and sobbing women, and while the solemn music sounds through all these vaults, and your pastor rises, struggling to control his own sorrow for the death of one he loved so well – O, may it be true, in that hour which is coming – may you begin from this night so to live that it shall then be true, that the mourners of that hour may sorrow here, not as those who have no hope, and that the men and women who honor you, and have gathered to pay honor to your memory, may feel like saying in simple sincerity as they look upon your coffin, "the memory of the just is blessed; let me die the death of the righteous and let my last end be like his." O begin today, God help you to begin from this hour of entrance into your new place of worship so to live that all this may be true when you pass away.

But one more thought. When was there ever any perfect worship? Once there was. There was a little obscure village; the military history of the country does not mention it; the older sacred writings do not. It was a despised village, and there was a lowly mechanic, who spent his early life in that village quietly, unpretending and unnoticed, and who used to go on the Sabbath day to the synagogue. He paid perfect worship. Oh, glorious, beautiful spectacle! He paid perfect worship, but since his day there has never been any perfect worship in this world. Shall there be any perfect worship for us then, who sometimes aspire towards God and long to worship Him in true spirituality, but never find the full attainment? God be thanked, we have hope of that higher and better life where we shall worship without effort and without imperfection. And God help us that we may strive to worship here with all our hearts, in the hope that at last we shall worship perfectly there.

Sermon One: The Blessing of Public Worship
Sermon Two: The Lord With Two or Three

Charles Haddon Spurgeon (1834-1892) is
undoubtedly the most famous minister of modern times.
Converted in 1850, he united with the Baptists and
very soon began to preach in various places. He became
pastor of the Baptist church in Waterbeach in 1851, and
three years later he was called to the decaying Park
Street Church, London. Within a short time, the work
began to prosper, a new church was built and dedicated
in 1861, and Spurgeon became London's most popular
preacher. In 1855, he began to publish his sermons
weekly; and today they make up the forty-nine volumes
of *The Metropolitan Tabernacle Pulpit*. He founded a
pastors' college and several orphanages. This sermon is
taken from *The Metropolitan Tabernacle Pulpit*, volume
41.

Charles H. Spurgeon

2

THE BLESSING OF PUBLIC WORSHIP

Two men went up into the temple to pray; the one a Pharisee, and the other a publican (Luke 18:10).

THIS IS CALLED A PARABLE; yet it is rather an incident, an anecdote, a statement of facts. You will observe that our Lord never used a fable. Fables may be employed to set forth that which is earth-born; but the parable, which is in itself true, is alone adapted to set forth spiritual truths. I say this just now because the other day, I read an assertion that the story of the rich man and Lazarus was only a fable, like that of Jotham. But the most of our Lord's parables are not only parables, but literal facts; and all of them might be facts. I would almost go the length of saying that all of them have been actual facts; and in this case there is nothing parabolic at all. It is the statement of an incident which did literally occur, for truth is best illustrated by truth; and as Christ had nothing to teach but what was pure truth, he illustrated it by truth, and never went into the realm of fiction, or invented a tale, or told a story which was not a fact, much less did he ever teach by a mere fable.

There were two men who went into the temple to pray, they prayed just in the way that our Lord describes, and they went away, the one justified, and the other without a blessing. Rather than the full teaching of the parable, I want to make a few observations.

It Is Well to Worship God in Public

I would say, first, that *it is well to worship God in public*: "Two men went up into the temple to pray."

It is good to pray anywhere. He who does not pray in his closet is but a hypocrite when he pretends to pray in the temple. Yet, though we pray in the closet, though we get into such a habit of prayer and are so full of the spirit of prayer that we can pray anywhere, yet it is well to go and mingle with others, and openly worship God, who delights to be thus worshiped. It was written very early in the history of our race, "Then began men to call upon the name of the Lord" (Gen. 4:26). It has been the custom of the godly to meet for worship in all times. The sheep of Christ are gregarious; this is their nature, they love to gather themselves into congregations, to feed in the same pasture, and to enjoy together the presence of their great Shepherd. It will always be so; the more pious and godly men are alone, the more will they love associated worship. If it should ever happily come to pass that each feeble one among us should be as David, and every David should be as the angel of the Lord, yet even then we should find strength and help in our service for God by meeting together for united worship. The apostolic command is, "Let us consider one another to provoke unto love and to good works: not forsaking the assembling of ourselves together, as the manner of some is; but exhorting one another: and so much the more, as ye see the day approaching" (Heb. 10:24, 25). Public worship is not everything; if there were no private worship, it would be nothing by itself. To go up to the temple is not everything. The man who does not meet God outside the temple will not meet God inside the temple, he may rest assured of that.

Yet, it is well, it is desirable, that it should be said of us as it was said of the men mentioned in our text, "Two men went up into the temple to pray." For public worship is, first of all, *an open avowal of our faith in God, and of our belief in prayer.* If we pray in private, nobody knows it; at least, nobody should know it, for our Lord's direction is very plain, "Thou, when thou prayest, enter into thy closet, and when thou hast shut thy door, pray to thy Father which is in secret; and thy Father which seeth in secret shall reward thee openly" (Matt. 6:6). Our acts of personal devotion must be sacred to God and our own souls; but when we go to the public assembly, whether it be but of two souls or three, or of many thousands, it matters not, there is to that extent an open declaration that we believe in God, that, let others do as they may, as for us, we worship Him, we believe in the reality and power and usefulness of prayer, and, therefore, in the light of day, before all men, we gather together to pray. I thank God that there is, in this unbelieving London, by so many thousands of assemblies of worshiping people, a public testimony constantly borne to the fact that we do believe in God, and that we do believe in prayer.

Public worship is also, in the next place, *a good way of securing unity in prayer.* A number of persons may agree to pray about one thing, yet they may never see each other's faces; their prayers may blend at the mercy seat, but they must lack an emphatic consciousness of unity such as we have who come together to pray. Our Lord Jesus promised his special presence to the united gatherings of his people when he said, "Where two or three are gathered together in My name, there am I in the midst of them" (Matt 18:20). Oh, dear friends, what would we do if we were not able to come together to mingle our sighs and cries and tears, and better still, to blend our joys, our psalms, our shouts of victory? As we are members of one mystical body, it is but right that we should, as members of that one body, worship together, lifting up the joyous song in tuneful harmony, and blending our supplications around our common mercy seat.

I think also that public worship is *a great means of quickening.* At any rate, it is so to me. I never feel that I can pray so well as when I am in the midst of my own dear friends; and, oftentimes, when things are flagging within the soul, to get together with brighter spirits, in whom the life of God is more vigorous, is a great help. It does not seem so very long ago—although these spectacles and my many gray hairs tell me that it must have been long since—that I used to say to my mother that hymn which begins:

> Lord, how delightful 'tis to see
> A whole assembly worship thee!
> At once they sing, at once they pray;
> They hear of heaven, and learn the way.

Dr. Watts put it very well, and I can utter the same sentiment,

> Lord how delightful 'tis to see
> This vast assembly worship thee!

Those two men, of whom our Savior spoke, did well to go up to the temple to pray; and we shall do well not to cease from the habit of assembling ourselves together for public worship in the Lord's house.

Then, dear friends, public worship is *a part of the great system by which God blesses the world*. It has much to do with the gathering, the sustenance, the strengthening, the invigorating, and the extension of the Church of Christ; and it is through the Church of Christ that God accomplishes His purposes in the world. Oh, the blessings that come to us in our public assemblies! Are there not, sometimes, days of heaven upon earth? Have we not felt our hearts burning within us when we have been listening to the Word, or joining in the praise or the prayer? Those houses of God where the gospel is truly preached, whatever the architecture may be, are the beauty and the bulwarks of the land. God bless them! Wherever the Lord's people are gathered together, in a cathedral or in a barn—it does not matter where—it is none other than the house of God, and the very gate of heaven when God is there; and who among us would dare to stay away? As long as we have legs to carry us, and health with which to use those legs, let us be found among the waiting assemblies in God's sanctuary.

For, once more, it seems to me that public worship on earth is *a rehearsal for the service of heaven*. We shall sing together there, not solos, but grand chorales and choruses. We shall take parts in the divine oratorio of redemption. It will not be some one melodious voice alone that shall lift up the eternal hallelujah. We shall all have to take our parts to make the harmony complete. I may never be able to rise to certain notes unless my voice shall be wondrously changed; but some other sinner, saved by grace, will run up the scale, nobody knows how high; and what a range of melody the music will have in heaven! I believe that our poor scales and modes of singing here are nothing at all compared with what there will be in the upper regions. There, the bass shall be deeper and yet the notes shall be higher than those of earth; even the crash of the loudest thunders shall be only like a whisper in comparison with the celestial music of the new song before the throne of God. John spoke of it as "the voice of many waters." The waves of one ocean can make a deafening, booming noise; but in heaven there shall be, as it were, the sound of sea on sea, Atlantic upon Pacific, one piled upon another, and all dashing and crashing with the everlasting hallelujahs from the gladsome hearts of the multitude that no man can number.

I expect to be there, and I remember that verse in one of our hymns that says:

> I would begin the music here, And so my soul should rise;
> Oh, for some heavenly notes to bear My passions to the skies!

But you cannot sing that heavenly anthem alone because, however well you can sing by yourself, that is not the way you will have to sing in heaven, there you will have to sing in harmony with all the bloodwashed hosts. Therefore, let us often come to the Lord's house; and when we are gathered together, let us again take up the words of Dr. Isaac Watts, and say:

> I have been there and still would go,
> 'Tis like a little heaven below.

That little heaven below shall help to prepare us for the great heaven above.

That is our first observation then. It is well to worship God in public.

Have a Purpose When You Worship

Secondly, *it is well to have purpose when we go to public worship.* "Two men went up into the temple *to pray.* They went there for that express purpose.

Now, whenever we go to the assembly of God's people, we should have some good reason, and the right one is that which these two men had. They went up to the temple to pray. I would rather that you came with a bad reason than that you did not come at all. I have known people come to pick pockets, and yet they have gone away with a blessing. I am sorry if any of you came tonight with that purpose, yet I am glad that you are here. Perhaps friends will prevent you committing the sin of theft by taking a little extra care of their pockets. I have known persons go into the house of God out of sheer mockery, and yet God has blessed them, for His ways are strangely sovereign. But that is to be ascribed to matchless mercy, and it is not the way we ought to appear before the Lord.

When we go to the sanctuary, we should go for a purpose, we should go to pray; *we should not go merely from habit*. Do we not often do that? Not so much on Thursday nights, I think, for people come then because they like to come; but on Sundays it is such a proper thing with certain persons to go to a place of worship that they almost wish it was not so proper, and they would like to have a good excuse for remaining at home. Well, if you come only out of habit, and you do not get a blessing, I pray you do not wonder at it. If you do not come for anything, and you do not get anything, do not be disappointed. If you go to a shop across the street, and do not mean to buy anything, do not be surprised if you come out without anything; and if you come here, and do not want anything, very well, you will go away with nothing. Is it not just what you might have expected? He who goes to the river, and takes no rod or net with him, will have no fish in his basket, even though there may be shoals of them in the water. So, if we want to be blessed in our worship, we must come with a purpose, even as these two men went up into the temple "to pray."

Neither do I think that we should come to the assembly of God's people *merely to hear sermons*. The proper thing is to come "to pray." "But we do hear sermons," says one. Yet, I hope that does not hinder your praying. Somebody said, the other day, that people who go to church go to pray, but that we who go to chapel go to hear sermons. My dear friend, that remark shows what sort of sermons you get at church, because those who come to hear us preach, pray while we are preaching, and they find that there is nothing that helps them to pray as much as a good sermon does. In fact, there is no worship of God that is better than the hearing of a sermon. I venture to say that, if a sermon be well heard, it puts faith in exercise as you believe it, it puts love in exercise as you enjoy it, it puts gratitude in exercise as you think of all the blessings that God has given to you. If the sermon be what it should be, it stirs all the coals of fire in your spirit, and makes them burn with a brighter flame, and a more vehement heat. To imply that hearing a sermon is not worship, is really to slander your minister. It must be a very bad sermon in which there is, as it were, a jerk out of the prayers to get into it, for the supplication should lead up to the sermons. And then the discourse should be a continuation of the prayer that has preceded it, and bring it back upon the mind again, so that all present may pray the better and worship God the more acceptably, because of the discourse to which they have been listening.

Still, if anybody comes to hear a sermon, especially as, perhaps, some of you came while I was away, to criticize the preacher, that is not the way to get a blessing. I do not mind if you criticize me. If we go to the house of God, and seek to turn the whole of the worship into a prayer, we shall not come away without a blessing. The main object in all worship is that we get near to God, and really pray to him.

Neither do I think that we should go to the house of God *merely to get comforted and cheered*. That is a very sweet result from hearing the Word; but it should not be our main object in going to hear it, we should meet together that we may draw near to God. If it be the Lord's will not to comfort but to rebuke us, and if it be his purpose not to cheer but to cast us down, we shall still feel, "What I received came from God. I prayed to him, and he spoke to me; and I had special fellowship with the living God, while I was also in communion with my brethren and sisters in Christ. That is what I went for."

The publican teaches us what we should go to the house of God to do and to say. There should be, in God's presence *confession of sin*. We should each one of us, when we draw near to the Lord, bow down in His presence with reverent awe. If the very angels veil their faces when they come near Him, we must humbly bow before Him when we come to worship in His house. He is in heaven, and we are upon earth. He is our Father, but He is also our Father who is in heaven; and we poor sinful creatures can never come into the light of His presence without perceiving that we are full of sin. I have heard some people talk about "walking in the light as God is in the light," as if that meant that they had no sin. Listen to what the apostle John says, "If we walk in the light, as He is in the light, we have fellowship one with another," and then "the blood of Jesus Christ His Son" is still needed, for even then it "cleanseth us from all sin." Without its continual application there would be no walking in the light; and the more walking in the light there is, the clearer will be the perception of every speck and stain in the character. So, the more true our worship is, the more certain shall we be to make confession of sin.

Communion with God and confession of sin should always be remembered by us when we come up to the house of God.

Then there should be *asking for mercy*. We should come as paupers seeking relief. We should come as rebels craving pardon. We should come as pardoned ones still asking renewed tokens of forgiveness; as men, once washed, who still come that their feet may be cleansed, that they may be clean every whit as they pursue their course on the journey of life.

In the publican's prayer there is, in the Greek, *a reference to sacrifice*. He cried, "Lord, be propitious to me the sinner." "Have mercy upon me for the sake of the great propitiation, the great expiation." They who come to God's house with a right purpose, come to find Jesus, to prove the power of His precious blood, to be perfumed with the incense of His all-sufficient merit, and to be covered with His matchless righteousness. That is the right way to come to the assembly of God's people, to speak with Him humbly, for we are sinful; prayerfully, for we are full of need; believingly, for Jesus has offered a sacrifice, and we are accepted in and through Him.

It is well to have a purpose when we go to public worship. I will just pause here and pass a few questions around for everyone to ask, "Did I come tonight with a definite purpose? Is that my general habit, to go to my place of worship with that purpose? Or do I go casually?"

Don't Forget the Purpose for Worshiping

Thirdly, *it is possible to go to public worship for a good reason, and yet to forget it*: "Two men went up into the temple to pray; the one a Pharisee, and the other a publican."

It was very remarkable that a Pharisee should forget his purpose; that is the one point concerning him to which I am going to call your attention. He went up to the temple to pray, and he did not pray. He never prayed a word, but he did something else. If it had been written "Two men went up into the temple to boast," I should give the Pharisee the palm, for he certainly did that magniloquently; but as it is said, "Two men went up into the temple to pray, then it is certain that this Pharisee quite forgot why he had come, for he never prayed at all.

Well, now, who was the gentleman that forgot his purpose? *It was the person who ought specially to have remembered it,* for he was a Pharisee. By profession he was a separatist from others because of his supposed peculiar holiness. He was a man amazingly acquainted with the Word of God, at least, with the letter of it. He wore some little black boxes between his eyes with texts of Scripture inscribed upon them, and he wore others around his wrist. He had very broad blue borders to his garments, for he was particularly observant of what he read in the law of Moses. And, generally, a Pharisee was a teacher; he was first cousin to a scribe, and often was a scribe himself. He had written out a copy of the law, and he had its precepts at his fingertips. Now, surely, if there is anybody who goes up to the temple to pray, this is the man who will pray. If anybody forgets why he came, it will not be this person. But, listen. That was the very man who did forget all about it; and this may be true of a minister, a deacon, an elder, one of the brethren who prays at prayer meetings, the leader of a Bible class, a teacher in the Sunday school, the best sort of people. "Oh!" you exclaim, "we cannot say anything but what is honorable of them;" and yet it was one of this class who forgot why he went up into the temple. Let me remind you church members who make a loud profession, that it was a great professor who went up to the temple to pray, and did not do it. What would you say to your boy, who went to a shop, and then came home, and said that he had forgotten what he went to get? And what will you say to yourself, dear friend, especially if you happen to be somebody notable, if it should be you who went up to the temple to pray, and did not pray? Oh, do not let it be so in your case; do not leave this church until you have had real fellowship with God, through Jesus Christ his Son!

How do we know that this man forgot his purpose? We know it by what he said. *He did not pray at all.* He said, "God, I thank thee, that I am not as other men are, extortioners, unjust, adulterers, or even as this publican. I fast twice in the week, I give tithes of all that I possess." By his words he must be judged, as you and I will be; and his words go to prove that he forgot why he went up to the temple. He acted as though he was in his own house, praising himself, instead of being in God's house, where the Lord alone is to be praised.   Why did this man fall into this great blunder, and forget why he went up to the temple? He did it because *he was so full of himself that there was no room for God in his heart*; he was so satisfied with himself that he felt no need of prayer. He already had all that he required, and he had so much that he could only stand still, and overflow with a kind of gratitude to the one to whom he owed everything, namely, himself. Though he said, "God, I thank thee," he did not mean it; he meant all the praise for himself. He was so fine a bird, and had such rich feathers, that he felt that everybody ought to admire him as much as he admired himself.

Well now, Christians, you will say to me, "Has this any bearing upon us?" Listen. Do you never feel perfectly satisfied with yourselves? Are there not times when there is no sin that burns the conscience, when you think you are somebody, a pattern saint, a highly experienced good old man, a rare Christian matron, and so on? The devil tells you all that, does he not? And you believe him. Or else you say that you are such a smart young man; you have only recently joined the church, yet you already are busy in the Lord's work in a wonderful way, there must be a great deal in you. You do not put this boasting into English, because we do not talk English to our hearts when we get proud; it is a sort of Greek which we talk, by which we try to conceal our own meaning from ourselves. Then we feel, perhaps, that we are getting perfect; that is the time when we forget to pray, and we go into the house of God, and, when we come out, we make some remark about the preacher's manner, or about Sister So-and-so, whose hat is really too gaudy for a Christian woman to wear, or about our friend So-and-so, who spoke rather roughly to us. We,—we,—we,—we are so good that we can find fault with all others, and say, "God, I thank thee, that I am not as other men are, or even as this publican;" and then we do not pray.

Whenever you get one inch above the ground in your own esteem, you are that inch too high. The way to heaven is down, down, down. As to self, it must sink; our sense of sin must grow deeper and deeper, and a sense of obligation to grace must be more and more fully impressed upon our hearts, until we are able to say with great emphasis, though it be in the deep silence of the soul, "God be merciful to me the sinner!" Otherwise, we shall come to the temple with the purpose of prayer, and we shall forget it; we shall go to the closet to pray, and yet shall not pray; or we shall read the Bible and not find anything upon which to feed our souls, because we are not hungry, but full. We shall not seek true wealth, because we shall fancy we are not poor, but rich; we shall not go to the source of all might, because we shall imagine we are not weak, but strong. If we go up to the temple as the Pharisee did, there will be nothing for us.

You Can Carry Out Your Purpose for Worship

So I close this sermon with a fourth observation. *It is*

possible to carry out our purpose in going to public worship. We can go to the temple to pray, and really pray.

Who is the man who is most likely to pray? According to this parable, it was the publican. *It was a man under a sense of sin.* It was a man who felt that he was *the* sinner, even if nobody else was *a* sinner. It was this man, to whom sin was a reality, not a fiction, and to whom the mercy of God was a real need, and not a mere doctrine, who craved that mercy at the throne, and felt that only sovereign grace could give it. It was this man who pleaded the precious blood of the propitiation, and felt that only by that way could he receive pardon. That was the man who truly prayed. Oh, have I not sometimes gone to pray with a breaking heart, groaning, and crying, and longing to see my Lord's face, and to have a sense of acceptance in the Beloved; and I have come away, and felt that I had not prayed, because I could not use language and words such as I would wish to use; and yet, on looking back, I have seen that it was then that I prayed most!

Next to the sense of sin, the publican had *sense of need.* When the need is felt the heaviest, prayer is truest. When the soul is lowest, then the flood of supplication is the highest. I am sure you pray best when you have least satisfaction with yourself, and you get nearest to God when you get farthest from self. When you feel that you are not worthy to lift up your eyes to heaven, it is then that heaven's eyes look down on you. The sorrowful thought of a broken heart is immeasurably better than the indifference of a callous spirit. Bless God for a humble mind that trembles at His Word; it is much better than that presumption which puts aside all feeling. There are some who will go to heaven questioning their own state all the way, yet they will arrive there safely; and there are some who never doubted of their state, who may have to doubt it when it is too late. Anyhow, it is a deep sense of sin, a deep sense of need, a deep sense of dependence upon sovereign grace, that helps a man to come to the house of God, and to go away with his purpose fulfilled.

Let us all try to bring our needs before God, let us sink ourselves in His presence, into the very depths, and then let us come and joyfully take what He freely offers to all who trust His dear Son. Let us receive grace at His hands, not as courtiers who have a right, but as those who feel like dogs under the table, and yet cry, "Lord even the dogs eat the crumbs that fall from the master's table" (Matt. 15:27).

The publican excites our pity, as we hear his groans and sighs, and see him smite upon his breast; but when we know that this is the man whom God blessed, and that he went to his house justified rather than the other, we no longer pity him, but we seek to emulate his repentance and his grace, and we pray the Lord to help us thus to come to His feast with a hearty appetite, thus to come to His wardrobe conscious of our own rags, thus to come to His fullness admitting our own emptiness, thus to come to the fountain of eternal life feeling that apart from it we are dead. Then shall we truly pray, even as this despised publican did.

Poor soul, almost in despair, you think, "I have no right to be here; I am so guilty, I am so vile." You are the very sort of sinner Christ died to save; not sham sinners, who have to pretend to be sinners, but you miserable sinners, you real sinners; not you who make marks on your skin, like some beggars do, that you may seem to be wounded; but you who are as bad as you can be, you who have sinned so deeply that you feel as if you were already lost, you who lie at hell's dark door, you who are dragged about by the hair of your head by the foul fiend of the pit, you who are in your own esteem the worst of all men. Come to Christ tonight. You are the people he came to save. He has come "to seek and to save that which was lost." Believe then that Christ died to save you, and you are saved. Throw yourself on His atoning sacrifice, and it avails for you at once. Glorify Him by trusting Him for your salvation. Let him be your High Priest, and from first to last your Savior; and He is yours as surely as you are a living man or woman. Go your way justified rather than the other who does not want the propitiation of the Lord Jesus Christ. The Lord bless you! Amen.

Sermon One: The Blessing of Public Worship
Sermon Two: The Lord With Two or Three

Charles Haddon Spurgeon (1834-1892) is
undoubtedly the most famous minister of modern times.
Converted in 1850, he united with the Baptists and
very soon began to preach in various places. He became
pastor of the Baptist church in Waterbeach in 1851, and
three years later he was called to the decaying Park
Street Church, London. Within a short time, the work
began to prosper, a new church was built and dedicated
in 1861, and Spurgeon became London's most popular
preacher. In 1855, he began to publish his sermons
weekly; and today they make up the forty-nine volumes
of *The Metropolitan Tabernacle Pulpit*. He founded
a pastors' college and several orphanages. This sermon
is taken from *The Metropolitan Tabernacle Pulpit*,
volume 41.

Charles A. Spurgeon

3

THE LORD WITH TWO OR THREE

Where two or three are gathered together in My name, there am I in the midst of them (Matt. 18:20).

WE HAVE IN the verses preceding the text a first mention in the New Testament of a *church meeting*. The Savior declares of His assembled people, "Verily I say unto you, whatsoever ye shall bind on earth shall be bound in heaven: and whatsoever ye shall loose on earth shall be loosed in heaven" (v. 18). A few believers, gathered out of the world, have met in the name of the Lord Jesus, to attend to the affairs of His household here below. It is a case of discipline. The meetings of God's servants for the necessary discipline of the church are not trifling meetings, but there is a divine power in them, since what they do is done in the name of Jesus Christ their Lord. Oh, that church meetings were more generally looked at in this solemn light!

Next, we are introduced to the *prayer meeting*. In verse 19, we read, "Again I say unto you, that if two of you," *two* of you, "shall agree on earth as touching anything that they shall ask, it shall be done for them of My Father which is in heaven." It is a very little meeting, it could not be smaller to be a meeting at all. There are only two there, but they are two praying men, and two believers. They are two of the Lord's own servants, whose great concern is His kingdom; they are two earnest persons who very greatly desire the prosperity of the church. They are two of kindred spirit, agreeing in love to God and the truth; they have talked over the matter, and considered it, and they feel moved by the Spirit of God to unite their supplications about one important subject. Will they meet together and pray in vain? As they are only two, will not the meeting fail to count with God? Assuredly not; the Lord Jesus Christ has aforehand left them this gracious promise, that if they shall agree on earth touching anything that they shall ask, it shall be done for them of His Father which is in heaven: they are only two, but this suffices to secure them the promised hearing.

The prayer meeting is not a farce, no waste of time, no mere pious amusement. Some in these times think so, but such shall be lightly esteemed. Surely they know not the omnipotence that lies in the pleas of God's people. The Lord has taken the keys of His royal treasury, and put them into the hand of faith. He has taken His words from the scabbard, and given it into the hand of the man mighty in prayer. He seems at times to have placed His sovereign scepter in the hand of prayer. "Ask Me concerning things to come: concerning My sons, command ye Me." He permits us to speak with such boldness and daring that we overcome heaven by prayer, and dare to say to the covenant angel. "I will not let Thee go except Thou bless me." If one Jacob can prevail over a wrestling angel, what can two do? What a victory would come to two who joined in the same wrestling! "One of you shall chase a thousand and two put ten thousand to flight." There is an accumulated power in united supplication: two do not only double the force, but multiply it tenfold. How soon the gate of mercy opens when two are knocking! God grant to each one of us a praying partner; when John pulls the oar of prayer let James join him in the hearty tug. Better still, may we always believe in our Father's presence at our prayer meetings, so that we may find the words of Jesus true when He says, "It shall be done for them of my Father which is in heaven."

Now, thirdly, we come to a promise in verse 20, which includes *every meeting of any sort* or kind which is for Christ's glory. So long as it is a sacred meeting of saintly men and women for the purposes of devotion or service — for the purposes of prayer or praise, or whatever else may be most suitable for the occasion, here is the promise for them — "For where two or three are gathered together in My name, there am I in the midst of them." This sanctions the church meeting for *worship* and this prospers the prayer meeting. Overshadowing every gracious assembly of the chosen we see the great Shepherd of the sheep, who here expressly says, "Where two or three are gathered together in My name, there am I in the midst of them."

Now, first, we shall mention with regard to these meetings, *matters not essential;* then, secondly, we shall carefully mention a *matter most essential;* and, thirdly, we shall dwell upon *an assurance most encouraging.*

Matters Not Essential

At the outset, we know that *numbers are not essential,* for "where two or three are gathered together in My name, there am I." It is very important in a large church that there should be large gatherings for prayer, for it would be an evidence of a slighting of the ordinance of united supplication, if a fair proportion of the members did not come together for that holy and blessed exercise. But, still, where that cannot be—where the church itself is small—where it is not possible for many to gather together—it is a very encouraging circumstance that numbers are not essential to success in prayer. "Where *two or three* are gathered together." The number is mentioned, I suppose, because that is about the smallest number that could make a congregation. We can hardly call it a congregation where the minister has to say, "Dearly beloved Roger, the Scripture moveth us in divers places," as we have heard was once done by a clergyman. Truly it was an assembly of two, and so was within the number, and under the circumstances might find the Lord present. But two out of a large church would have been a wretched sign of decline. If two were all that met out of a great church it would be a sadly little company, and the blessing might be withheld. Two or three are mentioned, not to encourage absence, but to cheer the faithful few who do not forget the assembling of themselves together, as the manner of some is.

Still, the number has this advantage, that it is the readiest congregation to be gathered. It is not difficult to make up two or three. A husband and wife: there are two. A husband and wife and a child: there are three. Or there may be two unmarried sisters, or a widow and child: two can be easily made up. Where there are no children, there may be a husband and wife and a servant: and these are three. Where there is no wife, perhaps there are two brothers, or a brother and a sister, or perhaps three sisters; and where there is no relation, but a man lives alone, it is possible to find one or two others with whom he can meet. It is a very handy congregation, because it can meet in a kitchen; it can meet in a closet: it can meet anywhere, for it is so small. It is also easily hidden away; in persecuting times two or three could get together in a corner, a cave, a cellar, or a garret. For that matter, two or three may be in prison together, and they can pray in one narrow cell; or they can do what Latimer and Ridley did when they stood back to back at the stake, and lifted up their hearts as one man. That was brave praying, when the two bishops stood to burn with devotion as well as to burn with fire for Christ's sake. I am sure that Jesus was in the midst of them when they met upon the faggots. Two people may meet in the street or in the field; they can get together in the corner of an omnibus or a train, and unite their supplications.

Today I commend to you the frequent practice of praying by twos and threes. There was a minister who had a little society which he called the "Aaron and Hur Society." It consisted of two—one to hold up his right hand, and one to hold up his left, while, like Moses, he was on the mount pleading for Israel. We want this institution multiplied to any extent. We want the twos and threes as well as the one separately praying, and then a blessing will come. But numbers are not important at all; we need say no more about them except this,—I like to note that the text puts it "two or three," for, as one remarks, that is much better than "three or two." For if "three or two" are gathered together, they are getting smaller; but if it be "two or three," they are evidently upon the increase. If they have only increased from two to three, they have advanced fifty percent., and that is something. If this congregation were to do that, where should we all be able to meet on Sunday for worship? On week nights I would encourage you to try to increase till we fill the upper gallery as well as the rest of the building. "Two or three." It is a growing congregation: but still numbers are not essential to God's presence.

Next, *the rank of the people is not important.* Does it say, "Where two or three *ministers* are gathered together in My name"? By no means. Ministers may expect the Lord to be in the midst of them, but they have no special promise as ministers: they must come before the Lord as plain believers. The "two or three" may be unable to utter a word by way of teaching the great congregation, but this is not mentioned in the promise. Does it say, "Where two or three instructed Christians, advanced in experience, are met together"? No, there is no such limit expressed or implied. In the matter of prayer or worship, no special boon is set apart for those who are eminent in grace. We do not read, "Where two or three *full-grown believers* are met;" much less does it say, "Where two or three *rich people* are met together." No distinction is made. If they are the people of God, and if they are the little ones whom the Lord has been describing, humble and lowly in spirit, where two or three of such are met together in the Redeemer's name "there," says Jesus, "am I in the midst of them." It may be that a poor man and his wife are praying together before retiring for the night. The Lord is there. A couple of servants unite their supplications in the kitchen. The Lord is there. Two or three little boys have come out of school, and they love the Lord, and so they have met in a corner to pray. The Lord is there. Do you remember how Luther was encouraged while he, and Melancthon too, were down in the dumps about the Lord's work? They were dreadfully downcast; but as Luther passed by a room, he heard the voices of children, and he stopped. Some women, the wives of good men, had gathered with a few holy children, and they were praying the Lord to let the gospel spread in the teeth of the Pope and all his friends. Luther went back and said, "It is all right. The children are praying to God. The Lord will hear them. Out of the mouths of babes and sucklings hath He ordained strength." So you see in the promise of the divine presence there is nothing said about *numbers*, and nothing about *rank*.

Neither is a word said as to *place*, except that it says "*where* two or three." "*Where*" means anywhere. In any place where two or three are met together in Christ's name there is He. Not in the cathedral only, but in the barn; not in the tabernacle only, but in the field. "Where" means everywhere. In the loneliest place, in the faraway forest, in an upper room, or on board ship, or in a hospital.

> Jesus, where'er Thy people meet,
> There they behold Thy mercy seat:
> Where'er they seek Thee, Thou art found,
> And every place is hallowed ground.

Anywhere Christ will be with you when you are with Him in prayer or in worship. Have you never read how the Covenanters, when the times of peace came, and they could worship in the church, yet, nevertheless, often looked back with sadness to the glorious days they had in the mosses and on the bleak hillsides when they were hunted by Claverhouses' dragoons, and the Lord covered them with the skirts of His garments? See the preacher reading his text by the lightning flash, and hear His voice sounding afterwards amid the thick darkness! The saints who had gathered together to hear the word of God had an overpowering sense of His presence which nothing could excel. Anywhere we may meet for prayer and worship and expect Jesus to be in the midst of us. The place is not essential even in the lowest degree. When I see people running out every morning to church, it savors of a superstition which ought to have died out long ago. When you look into the church you will find no great number assembled; generally the rector and one or two of the family make up the company. But if the whole parish came trooping out to church, I should say that they had better stay at home and pray with their fami-

lies. Family prayer is a better institution than the tin-
kling of a bell every morning, and the collecting of people
in a church. Have a bell of your own, and be your own
priest, and open your Bible, and pray yourself with your
children, and that will be a more acceptable sacrifice
than if you plod in your superstition half-a-mile to a so-
called sacred place to enjoy the voice of a supposed
priestly man. Dedicate your parlor; consecrate your
sitting-room; make your kitchen into a church for God:
for there is no sacredness in bricks, and mortar, and
stone, and stained glass. The outside of a church is as
holy as the inside. Far ought such an age as this to be
from the revolting superstition which makes the houses
of the godly to be common and unclean in order to mag-
nify the parish church. May we get back to the simplicity
of Christ! "Neither in this mountain, nor yet at Jerusalem, shall men worship the Father." The time is coming,
yea and now is, when in every place God seeketh spiritual worshipers who worship Him in spirit and in truth.

And will you please notice this, that as numbers and
rank and place are all non-essentials, so also is the *time*?
There may be—there ought to be to us from holy habit—
an hour of prayer. But though that be especially and
rightly the hour of prayer—for He that has no appointed
time for prayer may probably forget to pray—yet still
that pious custom must never degenerate into superstition, as though heaven's gate were opened at a certain
quarter of an hour, and shut during all the rest of the
day. Meet whenever you please, no time will be un-
seasonable. All hours are good, from twelve o'clock at
night to twelve o'clock the next night. The hour of prayer
is the hour of need, the hour of opportunity, the hour of
desire, the hour when you can come together. Let every
hour, according as occasion permits you, become the
hour of prayer. I have heard it said sometimes in the
country, "Well, we cannot get our people together for a
prayer meeting because they are busy at the harvest." If
the preacher were to get up at four o'clock in the morning, and hold a meeting for prayer out in the field itself
while yet the dew is on the grass, would it not be a capital

thing for him and for his flock? Suppose the people cannot come to pray at six o'clock in the evening, make it seven, make it eight, make it nine, make it ten. Perhaps the young folks had better be in bed at so late an hour, and there may thus be legitimate objections to some hours for public gatherings; but yet twos and threes may sit up as late as they like to pray, and no policeman will come round and tell them to go to bed. Our rulers do not ring the curfew now. The Lord our God doth neither slumber nor sleep; He is ever waiting to be gracious.

And, once more, there is nothing said here about *the form which the meeting is to take.* "Where two or three are met together in My name, there am I in the midst of them." "They are going to break bread together." Very well, they are quite at liberty to do so, and if they have met in the Lord's name, He will be in the midst of them. "But they are going to hear a sermon." All right: so they may. Preaching is an ordinance of God, and He will be in the midst of them. "But they are neither going to hold the communion, nor to hear a sermon; they are going to pray." Quite right; the Lord will be in their midst. "But they are not going to pray, that is to say, vocally; they are going to read a chapter, and sit and think of it." Quite right; the Lord will be in the midst of them. "But they are not even going to read, or sing, or pray vocally; they are going to sit still." The Lord will be in the midst of them if they meet in the name of Jesus. "Where two or three are gathered together in My name, there am I in the midst of them." We believe that *any form which true worship takes* is a form which the Lord Jesus Christ not only tolerates, but sanctions, if His Spirit be there. But if you meet without that Spirit of God, even though you should think yourselves infallibly correct in the form which your meeting assumes, that form will be of very little use to you. I bless God for the grand liberty of worship which is given here. I bless God that He has not laid down this regulation and that, but He has left His people to His own free Spirit. "Where the Spirit of the Lord is, there is liberty." Where two or three are gathered together in My name, there am I in the midst of them."

A Matter Most Essential

It is most essential that they should be gathered *in Christ's name*. Does not this mean that the gathering must be that of Christians met together as Christians to have fellowship with Jesus Christ and so with one another? Does it not mean that they must be met together in obedience to His will as they understand it, to carry out His will as they find it in the New Testament, and as the Spirit of God opens up that New Testament to them? Does it not also mean that they must be met together distinctly for the Lord's purposes?—to honor Christ, to bring glory to His name, to worship Him? They must be met together not to a kind of mystic, invisible, unknown Christ, but in His name, for Christ has a name—a distinct personality, a character; and that must be known, loved, and honored; or else we have not met in His name. Are we not to meet because He bids us meet, and because we have His authority for meeting, His authority for breaking bread, His authority for baptism, His authority for prayer, His authority for praise, His authority for the ministry of the word, His authority for reading the Scriptures, His authority for mutual edification? We meet not to carry out our own devices, but to carry out that which is appointed us by our Lord Himself.

And does not this gathering in His name mean that we are, first, to be known by His name, and then to get close to one another by drawing nearer to Him? The way to be gathered together is to be gathered by Him and to Him. If all press to the center, they all press to one another. If each man's aim be personal fellowship with Christ, personal knowledge of Christ, personal trust in Christ, personal adoration of Christ, personal service to Christ, and the getting of personal likeness to Christ, then we are all coming together. While our fellowship is with the Father, and with His Son, Jesus Christ, we also have fellowship with all the saints. This should be the great object of all our gatherings, to be brought more fully into Christ; and all of us must meanwhile believe that Jesus is in the midst and we must come together unto Him. You do not meet to listen to a certain preacher, but because through that preacher you have been helped to get nearer to the Lord Jesus Christ, and, therefore, you are glad to hear His voice, and glad to worship God with those friends with whom you have fellowship in Christ.

You do well to come where you have found Christ before; and you do well to stay away from any gathering wherein you have not found Christ. Some, as they go out of the place where they usually worship, are sadly compelled to cry, "They have taken away my Lord, and I know not where they have laid Him." Do not go where Jesus is not present; and if distinctly you are obliged to say, "I have heard sermon after sermon almost without mention of His name; I have gone for months together, and I have not had a sweet thought of heavenly fellowship arising out of the service"; then do not go there again. Do not go to any church merely because you have been in the habit of going. If your father used to live in Islington, but has now moved, you do not think it needful to go and call at his empty house, do you? Go where the Lord has met with you, and where you may expect that He will meet with you again. Sundays are too precious to be thrown away by sitting still to be starved. Even a cow does not care to be tied up in an empty stall, and a horse does not run to an empty manger. Seek the Lord Jesus, and do not rest till you find Him. We must gather in His name and get closer and closer to it, or else the Lord's day will run to waste, and barrenness will devour our souls.

An Assurance Most Encouraging

The last is the most important, and that is, — "Where two or three are gathered together in My name, there am I in the midst of them."

First then, briefly, *how is the Lord Jesus there?* Notice the exact words. Catch the gracious sense. He does not say, "I *will be* there," but He does say; "I *am* there." He is the first at the gathering; "Where two or three are gathered together in My name, there AM I." Not "I will be," though that is true; but He puts it in a more divine fashion, — "There am I." Jesus is there already before another arrives. He is the first in the congregation, the first comer in the assembly, and they come gathering to Him. He is the center, and they come to Him. "There am I."

How is He there? As we, His people, meet, He is there, because *He is in every one of them.* It is a blessed thing to see Christ *in* His people. Did you ever try to do that? I know some who try to see the old man in Christ's people. But, oh, to see Christ *in* His people—what a charming sight it is! And I think, with regard to every child of God that I know, that I can see a little more of Christ in him than I can see in myself. I cultivate the practice of endeavoring to see my Lord in all His people, for He *is* there, and it is irreverent not to honor Him. He *is* with them, and *is in* them; why should we doubt it? That is something worth remembering. If so many *temples of the Holy Spirit* come together, why, surely, the Holy Spirit Himself is there, and the place whereon they stand is holy ground. Jesus is in their thoughts, in their objects, in their desires; ay, and in their groans, in their sorrows, in their spirits, in their inmost souls. Where two or three are gathered together in His name, there is He in the midst of them.

And, next, *He is with us in His Word.* When the Book is opened, it is not mere words, it is the living and "incorruptible seed which liveth and abideth for ever"; and the Christ is in it as the immortal life, the secret life-germ in every seed that we sow. Christ is the *way*, if we teach men the road to heaven. Christ is the *truth*, if we preach the doctrines of grace. Christ is the *life*, if we enjoy and feed upon His precious name. Where His Word is preached, there He is; for it shall not return to Him void, but it shall prosper in the thing whereto He has sent it.

Christ is in His ordinances. He has not disassociated Himself from baptism, which is the blessed symbol in which His death, burial, and resurrection are clearly set forth. He has not separated Himself from that other ordinance, in which we behold His passion and see the way in which we become partakers of it, by feeding upon His body and His blood. He has promised to be with us

even to the end of the world in the keeping up of those
divine memorials of His incarnation and atonement, His
life and His death.

And then the Lord Jesus Christ is with the assembly
by His Spirit. The Spirit is His representative, whom He
has sent as the Comforter to abide with us forever. You
must have felt Him sometimes convincing you of sin,
humbling you, and bowing you down; then cheering you,
comforting you, enlightening you, guiding you, relieving
you, sustaining you, sanctifying you. Oh, what light He
brings! What life He brings! What love He brings! What
joy He brings! When the Spirit of God is in the midst of
God's people what merry days they have! What days of
heaven upon earth!

Does not this fact that Christ is among His people
show us that He must be divine? How can He be everywhere in all the assemblies of His people unless He is the
omnipresent God? We believe Father, Son, and Holy
Spirit to be one God; but Jesus Christ is God, and whosoever casts that truth away casts away eternal life. How
can he enter into heaven if he does not know Christ as
the everlasting Son of the Father? He must be God, since
He has promised to be in ten thousand places at one
time, and no mere man could do that.

Next, *where is the Lord in the assembly?* He has promised to be with His people; but where is He? "There am I
in the midst of them." Not up in the corner, but here in
the midst of them is the Lord. He is the center to which
all saints gather. He is the sun in the heavens lighting
all. He is the heart in the midst of the body giving life to
all the members. "In the midst of them." Is not that
delightful? The Lord Jesus Christ does not come into the
assembly of His people to bless the minister only. No,
you are all equally near in proportion to the grace of
nearness you have received. He is in the midst of you, in
the center of all hearts. Like the center of a wheel, from
which all the spokes radiate, Jesus Christ is the middle
of the company. Armies place the king or some great
general in the heart of the host, in the place of honor and
command; so, as our army marches to battle, our King is
in the center. The King is in the midst of the saints in all

His glory, and His presence is their strength and their assurance of victory. Glory be to our present Lord: He is in the midst of us now.

And if He is in the midst of His people, *what will He do?* Why, He is there to sanction every little gathering of His people—to say to the twos and threes, "You are not Dissenters, for you have met with Me. You are not Nonconformists: you are conformed to Me, and I am one with you. You are the Established Church—you two or three. I have established you in My everlasting love; those that meet in My name I have established them, and I have endowed them; and the gates of hell shall not prevail against them. I sanction your assemblies if you are My people." He is there *to bless* those who supplicate and adore. But, mark you, the text does not say this in so many words; and do not you say it, brother, next time you pray. Did I not hear you say, "Lord, Thou hast said, 'Where two or three are met together in My name, there am I in the midst of them, *and that to bless them, and do them good'"?* That last little bit is your own. That addition is not in the Bible, for it is not the Lord's way to say what never need be said. What other blessing do we want than Christ in the midst of us? If He is there, the blessing is not what He gives: but *He Himself is the blessing.* It is not what He does: *it is Himself.* It is not even what He says: *it is Himself.* Oh, blessed be His name for what He gives, and blessed be His name for what He does, and blessed be His name for what He says: but still more blessed be His name because He *Himself* loved us, and gave *Himself* for us, and now comes *Himself* into the midst of His people.

Now, if Christ Himself is in the midst of His people, He will bring us peace, just as He did when He dropped into the assembly of the eleven, the doors being shut. He stood and said, "Peace be unto you!" and when He had said that, He showed them His hands and His side. It was Himself, His own peace, and His own person which made His disciples glad. Then He said, "As My Father Hath sent Me, even so send I you." This was His own commission from His own lips to His own servants, and having said this, He breathed on them and said, "Receive ye the Holy Spirit." Thus His own breath and His own Spirit coming upon them made them strong for service, and that is what He means when He says, "I am in the midst of them."

Does not this make our meetings delightful – Christ in the midst of us? Does not this make our meetings important? How one ought to make an effort to be there! If we have met with Christ aforetime we shall not bear to be away. We shall long to meet Him again, and count it a great denial if we must be absent. Does not this make our meetings influential? The gatherings of God's people are centers of influence. When the gathering contains but two or three, if Christ is there, the eternal power and Godhead are present; and out of this Zion, the perfection of beauty, God hath shined. Where even two or three are met together, and He is in the midst of them, "There breaks He the arrows of the bow, the sword, and the shield, and the battle." He will make His power known, and the glory of His grace shall go forth out of those little companies even to the ends of the earth.

> Where two or three, with sweet accord,
> Obedient to their sovereign Lord,
> Meet to recount His acts of Grace,
> And offer solemn prayer and praise:
>
> There, says the Savior, will I be,
> Amid this little company.

"Oh, but," you say, "the pulpit is the great power of God, is it not?" I answer, it is so because of the prayers of God's people. One may speak, but what of that, unless the rest shall pray? Preaching is God's ordinance – His battle-ax and weapons of war; but, as far as the church is concerned, the arm that wields these weapons must be the prayer of the whole body of the faithful – the gathering together of the saints in the name of the Lord Jesus Christ. "Wherefore, forsake not the assembling of yourselves together, as the manner of some is," but come ye together as often as ye have opportunity, not neglecting other duties, but balancing them one with the other. He says, "Seek ye My face." Let your cry be, "Thy face, Lord, will we seek." When Sir Thomas Abney was Lord Mayor of London, in the middle of the banquet which takes place on the first night, he disappeared for a quarter-hour, and when he came back he said to the friends around him that he had been keeping a particular engagement with a most intimate Friend, and so he had retired for awhile. That appointment was to have family prayer with his household in the Mansion House, and that gathering for prayer he would not have given up on any account whatever. Say to all other things, "You must stand back, I have a particular appointment; I must meet the Lord Jesus Christ with two or three of His people. He says that He will be there, and I should not like Him to say, 'Where is My servant? Where is My son? Where is My daughter? Are they absent when I am here?'"

It is such a blessing to get to know the Lord Jesus personally. I heard the other day of a famous infidel, and agnostic,—that is, an ignoramus, a person who knows nothing,—and he went to a certain house to meet an elderly lady of considerable literary renown. He was told that she believed in the Word of God, and was a faithful follower of the Lord Jesus, so he thought that he would have a word with her before he went away. "Madam," he said, "I have been astonished to hear one thing of you. I hear that you believe in the Bible." "Yes, sir," she said, "every word of it." "And pray Madam," he said, "however came you to believe in that Book?" She replied, "One of the principal reasons that I have for believing in the Book is that I am intimately acquainted with the Author of it." That was a blessed answer. Faith gets to know Christ; and so, knowing Christ, and meeting Him in worship in the midst of His people, it becomes armed against all unbelief, and goes forth conquering and to conquer. So will it be with you, beloved, if you meet the Well-beloved alone in your closets, and if you add to this a regular attendance at the holy assembly. I pray you come, and make this house like heaven, which is thronged with shining ones who rejoice because Jesus is in their midst.

The Beauty of The Lord

John Daniel Jones (1865–1942) served for forty
years at the Richmond Hill Congregational Church in
Bournemouth, England, where he ministered the Word
with a remarkable consistency of quality and
effectiveness, as his many volumes of published
sermons attest. A leader in his denomination, he gave
himself to church extension (he helped to start thirty
new churches), assistance to needier congregations, and
increased salaries for the clergy. He spoke at D. L.
Moody's Northfield Conference in 1919. This sermon,
"The Beauty of the Lord", is from his book *The Hope of
the Gospel*, published in 1911 by Hodder and Stoughton.

John Daniel Jones

4

THE BEAUTY OF THE LORD

And let the beauty of the Lord our God be upon us (Psalm 90:17).

"THE BEAUTY of the Lord our God." It was Charles Kingsley, who was overheard in his last illness murmuring quietly to himself, "How beautiful God is! How beautiful God is!" Perhaps the phrase, "the beauty of God," strikes us as just a little inappropriate and incongruous. We do not often apostrophize God as Augustine did—"O beauty, so old and yet so new, too late I loved Thee." And yet it must be true that God is beautiful. He is indeed the supreme and absolute beauty.

The old Greeks put into their statues and representations of their gods their highest conceptions of human beauty; into their Aphrodite, all they knew of womanly charm; into their Apollo, all they knew of manly grace; into their Zeus, all they knew of royal majesty and dignity. The instinct that made them thus identify the divine with the beautiful was altogether right. It was only the mode of expression that was wrong. It was *physical* beauty they attributed to their deities, and they did this because their conception of deity was material and anthropomorphic.

But the Godhead is not like unto silver or gold graven by art and man's device. God is a Spirit, and the beauty that characterizes Him is moral and spiritual beauty. You cannot express this beauty on canvas or in stone, but you can always *feel it* with *the worshipful and believing heart.*

From this point of view—that is, from the standpoint of beauty of character—how beautiful God is! You could guess as much from glancing at His works. I remember a friend of mine, after reading a chapter from one of John Ruskin's works, remarking to me, "What a beautiful mind the man has!" And so exactly when I look out upon

the works of God's hands I always feel moved to say,
"What a beautiful mind God has!" Take the glory of the
springtide. The earth in springtime fills any one who has
any sense of beauty with a perfect exhilaration of
delight. It is full of light and fragrance and life and color.
I look upon the trees dressed in their new robes of fresh
and vivid green; I look upon the fields, decked as they are
with innumerable white-eyed daisies and yellow butter-
cups; I look at the wealth of color in our gardens; I listen
to the joyous song of the birds; and when I remember
that God is the Author and Giver of all this color, fragrance, glory and song, I am constrained to cry, with
Kingsley, "How beautiful God is! How beautiful God is!"
But though "nature," as our hymn puts it—

> With open volume stands
> To spread her Maker's praise abroad;
> And every labor of His hands
> Shows something worthy of a God,

it is not in nature that I find the highest revelation of the
"beauty of the Lord." For that I turn to the gospel. You
remember that passionate psalm in which the singer
expresses his love for God's house—"One thing have I
desired of the Lord," he cries, "that will I seek after, that
I may dwell in the house of the Lord all the days of my
life" (Ps. 27:4). And why did he desire this perpetual
abiding in God's house? He himself supplies the answer:
"To behold the beauty of the Lord." That was the attrac-
tion, the compelling fascination of the sanctuary—in it,
as nowhere else, the psalmist beheld the pleasantness of
the Lord, the delightsomeness of the character of God in
all its perfection and completeness. And to the psalmist
there was no vision comparable to this vision of the
divine pleasantness; everything else was dust and ashes
compared to this. Like Paul, he counted all things but
loss if only he could gaze upon God, and so he would fain
dwell in the house of the Lord all the days of his life, that
he might behold the beauty of the Lord. For it is in the
sanctuary that the "pleasantness," the "beauty" of God's
character is most clearly revealed. The heavens declare
the glory of God—yes, but His Holy Word declares it

more plainly still. And it is declared most plainly of all in the Incarnate Word—in Jesus Christ. If you want to behold the "beauty of the Lord," you can do better than study the book of nature; come and study Jesus Christ, for in Him dwelleth all the fullness of the Godhead bodily, and He and the Father are one.

Wherein the "Beauty" Consists

Now, I am going to ask the question: Wherein does the beauty of the Lord, as revealed in Jesus Christ, consist? For "beauty" is itself always a *product*. It is not itself a single quality or characteristic, it is the result of a combination of qualities and characteristics. It is so even in the matter of *physical beauty*. I cannot discuss beauty as an artist could. But this I know, that regular features by themselves do not create beauty; and a fair complexion by itself does not create beauty; and a graceful carriage by itself does not create beauty. Beauty is a complex thing. It takes regularity of feature, brilliance of complexion, grace of carriage, and, above everything else, pleasantness of expression to create the impression of beauty. It is like the ray of light. The ray is really not single, though it seems such. It is complex. Let it fall upon a prism and it splits up into its constituent colors. It is a combination of violet and orange and green and blue that produces the purity and beauty of the white ray. And moral and spiritual beauty is also a complex thing. It is never the result of one quality, but always a combination of qualities. Beauty is something that can be analyzed. You can see some of the necessary constituents of moral and spiritual beauty in most men's characters. But no human life ever lived on this earth has ever created the impression of perfect beauty. The combination is never complete. Some element is always lacking. There is always some defect, some flaw, some fault. The only perfect and flawless beauty is the "beauty of the Lord." Now, I want to inquire what are the elements that go to make up the divine beauty. What are the constituents which, blended together, create the impression of the divine "pleasantness"? I am not going to mention all of them, for every good we know of is in God. We will confine discussion to two qualities—contrasted qualities almost,—which, blended together, go far towards creating the impression of the ineffable beauty of God.

First, I will mention *God's holiness*. There can be no moral beauty without holiness. It is in a very real sense the basal, the foundation quality of all moral character. When a man's life is smudged and stained with sin, the beauty of his character is wholly gone. Now the Bible is full of an awestricken sense of the *holiness of God*. "The Lord our God is holy"—it was the first truth about the character of God that the Israelites were taught to learn. The contents of the law and the awe-inspiring circumstances that accompanied the giving to it were all meant to inscribe upon their hearts the truth of the "holiness of God." God is absolute, awful purity, that is almost the main lesson of the Old Testament. Before Him even the cherubim veil their faces in their wings and continually do cry, "Holy, holy, holy, is the Lord God of Hosts." So absolute is the holiness of God, that, compared with Him, even the whiteness of the angel's wing seems stained and soiled. And this quality of *holiness* is a permanent element in the beauty of the Lord. In Jesus Christ, He revealed Himself as the Holy One. Our Lord was the chiefest among ten thousand and the altogether lovely, and the basal element in His beauty is His holiness. "He did no sin, neither was guile found in His mouth" (1 Peter 2:22).

Perhaps in these days we are tempted to overlook, if not to ignore, this element in the divine beauty and glory. But there would be no beauty in God, He would indeed cease to be God, if He were not holy. The most striking feature in Swiss scenery, the glory and boast of Switzerland, is the vision of its mighty mountain peaks clothed in their mantles of snowy white. Take the snow mountains away, and you have destroyed the beauty of Switzerland. And in much the same way you destroy the "beauty of the Lord" if you forget His holiness. The basal thing in God's character is His "awful purity." We need to lift our eyes to these shining and snow-clad peaks of the divine holiness if we are ever to be moved to say, "How beautiful God is!"

And the second quality in the character of God that we'll consider is *His grace*. We've noted that *holiness* is the basal element in moral beauty. I must add that holiness in and by itself would not produce the impression of *beauty*. For the word "beauty" carries with it the suggestion of *charm*. Indeed, the word that is translated "beauty" might, perhaps, be more correctly translated "pleasantness." It is winsome and attractive beauty. It is not something that commands your admiration simply, it is something that constrains your love. Now, *holiness*, in and of itself, would scarcely constrain love. Nobody would think of describing those snow-clad peaks of Switzerland as "pleasant"—they are grand, if you like; majestic, if you like; awe-inspiring, if you like. And in the same way "holiness" by itself is not "pleasant"; it is too high and majestic and austere; it does not charm and win us; it awes us, it subdues us—I might almost say it terrifies us. "Woe is me, for I am a man of unclean lips" (Isa. 6:5), is the heart-broken cry of the prince of the prophets. It was a cry wrung from him by a vision of the holiness of God. "Depart from me, for I am a sinful man, O Lord," is the bitter cry of the chief of the apostles. It was a cry wrung from him by a vision of the holiness of God. There is something more than *holiness* needed to create the beauty that wins and charms and attracts. And that something more we find in God's *grace*. The holiness of God would compel our reverence and awe; but the grace of God wins our love.

That was what struck the disciples most about the character of Jesus. "We beheld His glory," says John; "glory as of the only begotten from the Father, full of grace" (John 1:14). It was this characteristic of Jesus that gave Him His charm. "Publicans and sinners," we read, "came together for to hear Him." It was His "grace" that attracted them. "The common people heard Him gladly."

It was His *love* that drew them. "The grace of Christ"—the stooping, condescending, love of Christ—how it shines forth in the gospel story! Read the account of the wedding at Cana,—what delicate *considerateness* Christ showed! Read the story of His visit to the house of Zacchaeus;—what infinite *compassion* and beautiful *hopefulness* He displayed! Read the narrative of His dealings with the woman who was a sinner—what a depth of *tenderness* and *forgiving love* He revealed! And these are the things that lent charm and winsomeness to the character of Jesus. No wonder the common people delighted to hear Him; no wonder publicans and sinners hung on His lips and followed Him from place to place—He was full of "grace." Mere holiness would not have drawn them.

Righteousness is apt to be hard and repellent. You remember what Paul says: "Scarcely for a righteous man will one die;" there is not much about the righteous man to command enthusiastic love. The righteous man is often harsh and austere. "But for a good man," he says, "some would even dare to die" (Rom. 5:7). When righteousness is blended with love to produce goodness, then men's hearts are won to such enthusiastic devotion that they will even dare to die. And that is what you find in Jesus—love has joined hands with righteousness to produce goodness. And Jesus Christ in this is but the picture and expression of God. God is more than infinite holiness; He is also boundless love. He is more than the pure God who cannot behold iniquity; He is the loving God who gave His Son to die to save the sinner. And that constitutes the beauty, the pleasantness, of the Lord; in Him mercy and truth have met together, righteousness and peace have kissed each other.

The Beauty of God, a Human Possession

And now, having briefly considered the "beauty of the Lord," I want to call your attention to the prayer the psalmist utters in the text. He prays, "Let the beauty of the Lord our God be upon us." He prays, in a word, that the divine beauty and glory may become the possession of all God's people. This is a daring prayer. Is it a possible prayer? Is it a prayer that can be answered and realized? Yes, surely it can. It was one of the best-beloved of our modern mystics who said in his own quaint way, "The Christian ought always to be good-looking." Beneath the quaint phrase there lies a great and blessed truth. The Christian ought always to be good-looking. He ought to share in the perfect beauty of God. "Let the beauty of the Lord our God be upon us." It is no vain and impossible wish. It is no foolish and unwarranted prayer. Men have shared in the glory of God. There have been men on whom, visibly and unmistakably, the beauty of God has rested.

The apostle tells us that all who steadfastly gaze upon the glory of the Lord are transformed into the same image from glory to glory. And the apostle's statement is confirmed and ratified by the facts of experience. Men have been so changed and transformed. "And they took knowledge of them," I read about Peter and John, "that they had been with Jesus." They had caught from their Master some of the "beauty of the Lord." "And all that sat in the council," I read about Stephen, "fastening their eyes on him, saw his face as it had been the face of an angel." Stephen had caught some of the "beauty of the Lord." "From henceforth let no man trouble me," said Paul; "I bear in my body the marks of the Lord Jesus" — "the marks of the Lord Jesus," not simply in the scars and wounds he had suffered in his Christian service, but even more in his consecration and devotion and absolute self-sacrifice; and all this was Paul's share of the "beauty of the Lord."

And to come from those early days down to these days of ours, there are men and women in our midst who are invested with this heavenly beauty. "I have seen God in you," a famous novelist makes one of her characters say of another; "I have seen God in you." The human life was glorified with some of the "beauty of the Lord." No, this is no wild, extravagant and impossible prayer. The "beauty of the Lord" is a beauty in which we may all share. The New Testament quite clearly contemplates our sharing in this beauty. In the beauty of *holiness*, to begin with, for Peter says, "Like as He which called you is holy, be ye yourselves also holy in all manner of living, because it is written, Ye shall be holy, for I am holy" (1 Peter 1:15, 16). And in the beauty of *love*, for Paul says, "Let this mind be in you which was also in Christ Jesus" (Phil. 2:5), and the "mind which was in Christ Jesus" was, as the apostle proceeds to show, the gracious, unselfish, loving and self-sacrificing mind illustrated in the Cross. The *grace* of the Lord Jesus Christ is to be with us.

The New Testament clearly contemplates our sharing in the holiness and love of God. The "beauty of the Lord our God" is to be upon us. But is it? Do we share in it? Have we some of the holiness of God? Do we participate, to some poor degree, in the divine purity? And have we the loving mind of Christ? And does the combination of holiness and love make people feel that the beauty of the Lord our God is upon us? I repeat once more, we may share in the very beauty of God; but, I am bound to add, it is not a beauty easily or cheaply won. This is a costly beauty, and it is not to be acquired without paying the price.

Holiness is costly. Every one who has sought to acquire it knows this. It costs struggle and agony and blood and tears. "We wrestle," says the apostle, "not against flesh and blood, but against the principalities, against the powers, against the world-rulers of this darkness, against the spiritual hosts of wickedness in the heavenly places" (Eph. 6:12)—that terrific struggle is the price of holiness. "If thy hand cause thee to stumble, cut it off; it is good for thee to enter into life maimed rather than having thy two hands to go into hell; and if thy foot cause thee to stumble, cut it off; it is good for thee to enter into life halt rather than having thy two feet to be cast into hell. And if thine eye cause thee to stumble, cast it out; it is good for thee to enter into the kingdom of God with one eye, rather than having two eyes to be cast into hell" (Matt. 18:8, 9). And this maiming and cutting, this lop-

ping off of the hand and the foot, this plucking-out of the
eye, represents the price and cost of holiness.

And if holiness is *costly*, so also is the *grace of love*. See
what it cost God! It cost Him His only Son. Calvary
stands for the cost of love to God. And Calvary stands
forever as the type and illustration of the costliness of
love. For *love* implies a cross and a crucifixion. Love
implies the crucifixion of self, the absolute putting away
and annihilation of self. Therefore Jesus said, "Whosoever would come after Me, let him take up his cross,
deny himself daily and follow Me" (Matt. 16:24). The
cross—that is the price of love. Yes, without doubt, this is
a costly beauty. But it is worth the price. All other
beauty is like a fading flower. Age wrinkles the fairest
brow, takes the color out of the brightest cheek, bends
the straightest and most graceful form; but age cannot
wither "the beauty of the Lord." It grows ever more and
more beautiful as the years pass. The only change is a
change "from glory to glory." And it ends in the perfect
and complete beauty of heaven. "We shall be like Him,
for we shall see Him as He is" (1 John 3:2). I ask, once
again, do you possess this fadeless and heavenly beauty?
Physical beauty is beyond the reach of many of us; but
"the beauty of the Lord our God" may become the possession of all of us. If we commune with Christ, if we take up
our cross and follow Christ, we shall be transformed into
His image from glory to glory.

The Effect of This Beauty on the World

In the last place, notice the effect of *the divine beauty
upon the world*. If only the beauty of the Lord our God is
upon us, the world will be startled, charmed, subdued.
There is no such apologetic for Christianity as a beautiful Christian life. A holy and loving character is the most
potent and effective of all sermons. Perhaps that is why
Christianity has made such slow progress; there has
been so little of the beauty of the Lord our God upon us.
There has been so little holiness; there has been so little

love. There has been so little difference between us and men of the world. We have been selfish, grasping, loveless, as they are. The world is so indifferent to the charm of Christianity because it has seen so little of it. But whenever people see Christian folk with some of the beauty of the Lord upon them, they are subdued and won.

I read about the members of the early Church, in the spirit of love, selling their goods and contributing to one another's needs, continuing steadfastly in the prayers and taking their simple food with gladness and singleness of heart, praising God; and the result of it all was "they found favor with all the people." All Jerusalem was impressed by the vision, in the characters of these first Christians, of "the beauty of the Lord." I read about a young Glasgow engineer who joined a Glasgow church, and who, when asked what it was that had won him for Christ, replied that it was the impression produced upon him by the life and character of the foreman in his shop. He had been won by the "beauty of the Lord" in a human life. And that is what I believe is most sorely wanted in order to conquer the world for our Lord—that the beauty of the Lord our God should be upon all of us.

A significant sentence follows this one of the text: "Let the beauty of the Lord our God be upon us: establish thou the work of our hands upon us; yea, the work of our hands, establish thou it" (Ps. 90:16). That is a striking sequence—*first* the "beauty of the Lord," *then* "the established work." *First* the Christian character, *then* the success of our labors. We cannot have the second without the first. There can be no triumph for the Christian church until all Christians are clothed in beauty of the Lord. But if only the beauty of the Lord were upon us, our work would be speedily established. "If those who call themselves Christians only lived the Christian life," said Charles Kingsley, "the world would be converted to God in a day." We long to see our work established; we long to see church and school crowned with success; we long to see the kingdoms of the world becoming the kingdoms of our God and of His Christ. But there is a prior prayer we need to offer. The secret of the slow progress is in ourselves. We are such unlovely Christians. We do not commend the gospel we profess. Let us ask God to do His work first upon us—to purge us of our littlenesses and selfishnesses and sins, to make us holy and pure and loving. Yes, let us pray that, whatever the price and cost, "the beauty of the Lord our God" may be upon us; then will God also establish the work of our hands upon us; yea, the work of our hands He will establish it.

Sermon One: The Relevance of Worship to Life
Sermon Two: Our Duty to Praise

James S. Stewart (1896–   ) pastored three
churches in Scotland before becoming professor of
theology at the University of Edinburgh (1936) and
then professor of New Testament (1946). But he is a
professor who can preach, a scholar who can apply
biblical truth to the needs of the common man, and a
theologian who can make doctrine both practical and
exciting. He has published several books of lectures and
biblical studies, including *A Man in Christ* and *Heralds
of God*. His two finest books of sermons are *The Gates of
New Life* and *The Strong Name*. This sermon is taken
from *The Wind of The Spirit*, published in 1941 by
Abingdon Press, Nashville and New York.

James S. Stewart

5

THE RELEVANCE OF
WORSHIP TO LIFE

The four and twenty elders and the four living creatures
fell down and worshiped God that sat on the throne, saying, Amen; Alleluia (Revelation 19:4).

WE HAVE COME in to this sanctuary today to worship
God. The world around is full of wars and rumors of
wars, and no one knows what may be coming on the
earth; but we are here today to worship God. We have
come to this place along very different roads of circumstance and experience. I suppose that no two roads that
we have travelled through life have been quite identical,
but here we are today to worship God. Perhaps the
journey has not been easy for some of us recently. We
have been having to cope with difficulties and problems
and forebodings and disappointments and temptations.
Perhaps life has been besieging us with its complexity,
battering us with its fierce enigmas: the ways of providence have seemed mysterious and dark and difficult to
understand. As George Meredith expressed it:

> Ah, what a dusty answer gets the soul
> When hot for certainties in this our life.

But at any rate here we are today to worship God.

And the question is: What ought this worship to mean
for us in our actual life situation? Shall we be happier,
stronger, more resolute, more serene for having paid our
vows to the Lord this day in the midst of His people? But
let there be no misunderstanding, I am not suggesting
that the main object of worship is the effect it may
produce on the worshipers. Its object is God, its sole aim
His glory. But we want to see just where and how worship and life impinge together; and this, without any
descent into a false subjectivism, we are certainly entitled to ask. When we leave this place, what spirit ought

our worship to have kindled within us as we go out to face life and all its crowding, clamorous perplexities again?

To this question Charles Wesley, in that great and moving hymn which surely goes to the very heart of Christian worship:

> Let saints on earth in concert sing
> With those whose work is done;
> For all the servants of our King
> In earth and heaven are one—

and John in the book of Revelation have a very dramatic answer. It is not the kind of answer we might have expected, but it is all the more arresting on that account. It is this: if you want to learn anything about worship and its relevance to life, try to overhear the worship of the saints in heaven. The church militant on earth must capture for itself the essential notes of the worship of the church triumphant.

"I heard," writes John—and, mark you, he was not idly dreaming on a day of summer ease and spiritual complacency (he would have had nothing to say to us in this grim, tragic age of ours if that had been his background); no, he was writing when the shadow of the devilry of the emperor Domitian was on the world, when withering blasts of militant atheism were scorching the earth and the empire was running red with martyred blood, when no Christian's life was worth a moment's purchase and John himself was a prisoner in the mines and in the concentration camp on the island of Patmos—"I heard," he declares out of that background, "the echo of the worship of the redeemed in heaven: they fell on their faces before the throne of God, and cried 'Amen! Hallelujah!'"

Two words. You know what these words mean. "Amen"—so let it be! God's will be done. "Hallelujah"— praise ye Jehovah, praise the Lord most mighty!

John brought that majestic vision of the heavenly worship back with him. Why? In order that the church on earth, the poor, frail, persecution-battered church he knew, should learn for its own worship something from the worship of its friends in glory; in order that the Magnificat of heaven should not be quite unknown on earth in days of darkness and confusion.

> Some day or other I shall surely come
> Where true hearts wait for me;
> Then let me learn the language of that home
> While here on earth I be:
> Lest my poor lips for want of words be dumb
> In that high company.

So let us listen to it now. Amen! Hallelujah! Two words—and in these two words four notes are present, the *four notes* which together make up the harmony of worship and the victory of faith.

Acceptance of the Will of God

The first essential note of worship in its relevance to life is the *acceptance of the will of God.* This is the first characteristic attitude of the soul that worships in spirit and in truth. They stand before the throne and say, "Amen. So be it, Lord!"

John means that those who have passed over to the other side, whatever they may have suffered here on earth, have no rebellion now within their hearts. Here in the thick of the battle it may be difficult to understand; but away yonder in the perspective of eternity they have seen the plan complete. For them the Master's word is verified: "What I do thou knowest not now, but thou shalt know hereafter." And today they know, and are content. "Just and true are all Thy ways, Thou King of saints!" Amen—so let it be!

So they cry back to us from the sunburst of eternity that all is well. And one day, please God, we shall know it too.

But we have to learn it here. And this is where worship can come in decisively to help us. This is where worship and life are linked inextricably together. It can be so difficult, so terribly difficult sometimes, amid the personal strains and complications and lonelinesses and frustrations and griefs of life, to bow submissively to the will divine.

I know there are some who dislike the very sound of such words as submission and resignation. There is a youthful immature theology that would banish them from its vocabulary. "Resigned? Why should I be resigned? That is weak and feeble and sub-christian. Am I to accept the ills of life, and sit submissively with folded hands, and drug my soul to sleep? God forbid!"

All honor to that gallant rebel mood. But–and this is the point–do not let us forget that if there is a false and feeble pseudo-pietistic way of submitting, there is also an acquiescence that is true and beautiful and brave and Christlike.

"O My Father," prayed Jesus with the red agony of Gethsemane on His brow, "if it be possible let this cup pass. Nevertheless not My will, Father, but Thine! Thy will be done. Amen–so let it be" (Matt. 26:39).

But we? No. We are different. We see some grim darkness threatening, or some potential catastrophe descending on our dreams, and we want to cry, "Don't permit that, God! Never allow it. I couldn't stand it!"

There was a day at Caesarea Philippi when Jesus took the disciples into His confidence. His hour, He told them, had come. He was about to make the supreme sacrifice on the battlefield of the world. It was His Father's will, and He could do no other. Quietly and gently, yet firmly and inexorably, He told them what must be. All of a sudden Peter, listening, and struck cold to the heart by that frightful prospect of losing his Lord, strode up to Jesus. "Master, this shall not be unto Thee! I refuse to say Amen to it. God's will or not God's will–this shall not be!" And if we had belonged to the disciple group then and in the days that were to follow, I imagine we should have said and done the very same. "Come down from that cross, Jesus! There cannot be any will of God in this. Come down!" And then the world would have remained unsaved for ever. "The cup which My Father hath given Me, shall I not drink it?"

And we must learn to say it too. Even when life brings

us to the breaking-point, and hurts us fiercely with its cruel enigmas, we must learn to say it too: Amen, so let it be.

Now in worship we do at least begin to learn it. For it is through worship we come to know that there is just one thing needful at such a time. It is to possess Christ. It is to be sure that there beside you in the dark is One who still, as in the days of old, gathers the lambs with His arm when they have been hurt, yes, even when in their foolishness they have hurt themselves, and carries them in His bosom. O dear, kind Shepherd, Christ, the darkness is not dark with Thee, but the night is clear as the day!

Which of the two ways is ours? When proud Cleopatra of Egypt faced the wreck and ruin of her hopes, "It were for me," she cried in bitterness, "to fling my scepter at the injurious gods, since they have stolen my jewel!" That is one way. But there is another; and if you have ever lost a loved one or said good-by to hope, will you listen to this of William Barnes, the Dorset poet?

> Since I do miss your voice and face
>   In prayer at eventide,
> I'll pray with one sad voice for grace
>   To go where you do bide;
> Above the tree and bough, my love,
>   Where you be gone afore,
> An' be awaiten' for me now,
>   To come for evermore.

Commitment to the Purpose of God

If the first essential note of worship in its relevance to life is the acceptance of the will of God, the second is the *commitment to the purpose of God*. This also was in the "Amen" John heard across the battlements of heaven. For in this same chapter he has a vision of the exalted Christ riding forth to the conquest of the world, and all the saints in glory streaming out after Him on that high crusade. They rest not day or night. They follow the Lamb wherever He goes. For them the divine purpose means action fuller and service grander than they ever knew on earth. Amen, Thy will be done—*and help us to do it*. This is the meaning.

And through our worship we must learn this too. For Christianity is not all submission and resignation, though Marx and Nietzsche thought it was: "a slave morality," said Nietzsche; "the opiate of the people," said Marx and Lenin. Blind fools, had they not read history? Had they not seen the risen Christ in every age inspiring action and energy and courage unsurpassed? No doubt— let us confess it—part of the blame for the misunderstanding must lie at the door of the Church itself. For too often Christians have allowed the faith to appear as a reactionary influence in a revolutionary world; whereas the truth is the exact reverse. It is secularism that is reactionary; Christianity, when authentic, is revolutionary enough, as the Book of Acts reminds us, to "turn the world upside down." And indeed, all through the centuries, in the name of Christ men have marched right up to some of the most formidable, virulent social evils, crying, "It is not the will of God that we should tolerate this hateful tyranny one moment longer; it is the will of God that we destroy it!"—and there and then the axe has been laid to the root of the noxious tree, and the hideous abuse has crashed to its destruction.

For the *will of God is* not simply something to be accepted and borne—it is something *to be asserted*, something to be done. And Amen is not always a sigh; it is sometimes a shout:

> My God, my Father, make me strong,
> When tasks of life seem hard and long,
> To greet them with this triumph song:
>   Thy will be done!

Where this note is lacking, there is no true worship.

There was a day when David, having brought up the ark to Jerusalem, summoned his people to a new campaign, and told them of the wonderful destiny to which the Lord God of their fathers was now calling them; and the magnificent passage in Chronicles ends with a sudden irrepressible shout from the whole congregation— "All the people said 'Amen,' and praised the Lord" (1

Chron. 16:36). I can imagine the sound of that great "Amen" reverberating around the hills and making the Philistines tremble! If we would only say "Amen" to our own prayers, which means putting ourselves into these petitions, backing up our supplications with the resolution of dedicated lives—"Thy Kingdom come: *Amen!* Thy world be swept clean of war and oppression and racial discrimination and injustice: *Amen!* Bless our foreign missions: *Amen!*"

> Move o'er the waters' face
> Bearing the lamp of grace,
> And in earth's darkest place
> Let there be light.

Amen!"—if we would say "Amen" to our own prayers by thus putting heart and mind and will at Christ's disposal, we should go out and crusade for Christ as we have never done before.

This is urgent. For today there are men and communities and nations saying "Amen" with all their soul to false God-denying philosophies and ideologies, saying it with a mystic fervor and passion. There are nihilistic creeds that have great multitudes of flaming, dedicated missionaries. Will not we Christians then say "Amen" to the purpose of our heavenly Father—until every Christian is an instrument in the hand of God, every Church member a missionary for the Kingdom of Christ? There is so much land yet to be possessed. There are so many radical reformations still to be achieved, so much shame of war and cruelty and poverty and ignorance and racial bitterness still to banish from the earth.

"What think ye of Christ?" cries Browning in one place,

> You like this Christianity or not?
> It may be false, but will you wish it true?
> Has it your vote to be so if it can?

What a day this would be for the Church if the "Amen" of faith and devotion were really a shout of consecrated self-commitment: "It has my vote! I am in this unreservedly. Lord, here am I, send me, Amen!"

Joy in the Fellowship of God

We pass to the third essential note of worship in its relevance to life. For through acceptance of the will of God, and commitment to the purpose of God, there comes a wonderful sense of *joy in the fellowship of God.* "I heard," says John of the Revelation, "the worship of the Church of heaven, and it was Amen—but it was more: it was Amen, Hallelujah!" For yonder where they dwell in Christ they are eternally happy, and all their sufferings and sorrows of this earth are swallowed up in gladness and felicity. "In Thy presence is fulness of joy; at Thy right hand there are pleasures forevermore" (Ps. 16:11). And if we have lost this note—and who can deny that many of us have lost it?—it is through worship that we must recapture it.

It is a very extraordinary fact that all the way through this Book of Revelation, which was written at a time when Christianity was fighting for its very life, and Christ had His back to the wall, and the little flock of Christ was being battered with hideous atrocious cruelties and colossal sufferings, there breaks irrepressibly the sound of singing.

But that is just Christianity all over. "What is faith?" cried Tertullian in the third century, and answered his own question: "Faith is patience with the lamp lit." That is a lovely word, worth inscribing on the front page of your private Bible. For this is where the Christian has the stoic and the cynic and the fatalist utterly and forever beaten. Patience is stoic: patience with the lamp lit is Christian. The stoic may talk grimly about taking fate by the throat; the cynic may shrug his shoulders and say he "couldn't care less." But it is a different trumpet-note you meet on every page of the New Testament. Here are men, to use their own words, "glorying in tribulation," "enduring longsuffering with joyfulness." Here is not only "praise to the Holiest in the height"; here is also "and in the depth be praise!"

But far too much we have lost it. Burne-Jones was present at the funeral service for Robert Browning. But he said afterwards that it was too somber for his liking. It did not seem to fit the gallant soul whom they were remembering. "I would have given something," said Burne-Jones, "for a banner or two; and much would I have given if a chorister had come out of the triforium and rent the air with a trumpet." Far too much the Christian Church has lost that lyrical note. "How shall we sing the Lord's song in this strange land?" we complain. "What room is there for hallelujahs in this disillusioning desert of an age, this fierce, mad, bitter Babylon of a world?" "By the rivers of Babylon, there we sat down; yea, we wept, when we remembered Zion" (Ps. 137:1).

But I recall a day at St. Andrews when I was acting as chaplain to a student conference—very vividly do I remember. It was shortly after the end of the war, and there came to us for one night of the conference that great leader of the church in Holland, Dr. Hendrik Kraemer. He had spent some terrible months as a prisoner in a concentration camp and his face was lined with suffering. He spoke to these young students that night for half an hour, and the whole burden of his message was this: "We Christians must get the joy of Christ back into our religion. We are denying Christ by losing it!"

And certainly real Christians do seem to capture it, don't they?

> What is this psalm from pitiable places,
>   Glad where the messengers of peace have trod?
> What are these beautiful and holy faces
>   Lit with their loving and aflame with God?

There was a modern martyr of the church, James Hannington of Oxford and Uganda. He was consecrated Bishop of Eastern Equatorial Africa, and toiled there shiningly for Christ until his work was cut short by violent death. "I felt," he wrote in his diary just before the end, "that they were coming upon me to murder me; but I sang 'Safe in the arms of Jesus,' and laughed at the agony of my situation." That is apostolic and Johannine—safe in the arms of Jesus, and laughing at the agony!

"I heard," says John, "the voice of the saints of God; and it was Amen! Hallelujah—praise the Lord!" And I pray that even our worship today may help to bring the joy of Jesus back to some disconsolate heart.

But now, what is the deep root of this joy which can sing its Hallelujahs through the darkness? Here we reach the fourth essential note of worship in its relevance to life, the final characteristic attitude of the soul that worships in spirit and in truth.

Assurance of the Victory of God

John, Tertullian, Hannington and Kraemer were not deluding themselves with rhetorical fantasies and vague emotions. They were not whistling to keep their courage up in the dark. They were rejoicing—John reiterates it all through his book—because of something which had actually happened in history. There has been an advent, says John. There has been a Cross. There has been a Resurrection. God in Christ has met the powers of darkness at their worst. He has taken their measure, and has triumphed. Nothing has been left undone. Once and for all, atonement has been achieved and death destroyed, and the doors of the kingdom of heaven flung open wide. Once and for all, God has devised for this ruined world a way out of chaos and damnation. Therefore, be not dismayed! You are fighting a defeated enemy. This is the fact that cannot be shaken. This is the rock of God beneath your feet.

> Thou hast redeem'd us with Thy blood,
>   And set the pris'ners free;
> Thou mad'st us kings and priests to God,
>   And we shall reign with Thee.

Some fifty years after John wrote his book, there was a frightful martyrdom in the city of Smyrna, during the proconsulship of Statius Quadratus. The aged Polycarp, bishop and saint, was brought to his trial. His judge stood before him and cried, "You are to renounce the faith! You are to curse the name of Christ!" But Polycarp answered, "Fourscore and six years have I served Him, and He never did me wrong. How then can I revile my King, my Savior?" So they took him and burned him to death in the amphitheatre. But the young church in Smyrna hurled its defiance in the very face of his murderers; for when later it came to write down in the annals of the church what had happened, it was very careful to put in the precise date, and it gave it thus; "Polycarp was martyred, Statius Quadratus being proconsul of Asia, *and Jesus Christ being King forever!*"

Do let us believe our faith wholeheartedly. God so loved the world. Christ died for our sins. He is risen and alive forever. He has sounded forth the trumpet that shall never call retreat. The kingdoms of this world are become the Kingdom of our Lord and of His Christ, and He shall reign forever and ever. He is the way, the truth and the life. Whatever our moods of callow skepticism and agnosticism may say, these things stand impregnable and secure. This is the Lord's doing. This is the victory. Surely, then, we of the Church militant who are struggling here on earth and finding the battle often stern and hard and the road much rougher than we hoped, surely we can lift up our hearts amid the shadows and join our voices today with the Church triumphant, and with our own loved ones across the river who are forever singing the praises of their Redeemer: "O Jesus, King most wonderful, gathering even now Thy Kingdom to Thyself, Thy will be done! Thy praise be sung!" Surely we can say it: Amen, Amen! Hallelujah, Hallelujah!

And to His dear name be the glory.

Sermon One: The Relevance of Worship to Life
Sermon Two: Our Duty of Praise

James S. Stewart (1896–   ) pastored three
churches in Scotland before becoming professor of
theology at the University of Edinburgh (1936) and
then professor of New Testament (1946). But he is a
professor who can preach, a scholar who can apply
biblical truth to the needs of the common man, and a
theologian who can make doctrine both practical and
exciting. He has published several books of lectures and
biblical studies, including *A Man in Christ* and *Heralds
of God*. His two finest books of sermons are *The Gates of
New Life* and *The Strong Name*. This sermon is taken
from *The Gates of New Life*, published in 1928 by T. &
T. Clark, Edinburgh.

James S. Stewart

6

OUR DUTY OF PRAISE

Praise ye the Lord. Praise the Lord, O my soul. While I live will I praise the Lord. I will sing praises unto my God while I have any being (Psalm 146:1, 2).

ALL THE WAY through the Book of Psalms, even in its most sorrow-laden passages, you feel that you are walking on a smoldering volcano of praise, liable to burst out at any moment into a great flame of gratitude to God. And as the book draws to its close, the flame leaps clear from the smoke: here you have praise, and nothing but praise.

You have perhaps watched a great conductor bringing every member of his orchestra into action towards the close of some mighty music, you have seen him, as the music climbed higher and higher, signaling to one player after another, and always at the signal another instrument responding to the summons and adding its voice to the music, until at the last crashing chords not one was left dumb, but all were uniting in a thrilling and triumphant climax. So these final psalms summon everything in creation to swell the glorious unison of God's praise. They signal to the sun riding in the heavens, "You come in now, and praise Him!"—then to the myriad stars of night, "You now, praise Him!"—then to the mountains, raking the clouds with their summits, "Praise Him!"—then to the kings and judges of the earth, "Praise Him!"—then to young manhood in its strength and maidenhood in its grace and beauty, "Praise Him!"—then to the multitude of saints in earth and heaven, "Praise Him!"—until the wide universe is shouting with every voice the praise of God alone. "While I live," cries the psalmist, "will I praise the Lord: I will sing praises unto my God while I have any being."

Now that is religion. That is the test of religion. Wherever you have real religion, be sure of this—the domi-

nant note will be praise. That is why, when you come
down the centuries to Christianity, you find that there is
more praise in it than in all the other religions of the
world put together.

Some religions are not strong in praise. They have
very little if any song about them at all. Mohammedanism, for example. Mohammedanism knows how to
wield the scimitar; it does not know how to strike the
harp. Or Stoicism. The Stoic creed is great and noble
and rugged in endurance; but it is poor and dry and
barren in song. Or Puritanism of a certain stamp–not
the splendid, positive Puritanism of Milton, Cromwell,
and Bunyan, but the negative, reactionary, repressive
Puritanism of which Edmund Gosse, for instance, gave
such a memorable picture in *Father and Son*–that is
religion without a note of praise about it. But what
makes Christianity, what differentiates Christianity, is
the sounding out all the way through it–even in the
tears and anguish of it–of the one diapason note, praise
to God. "While I live," says this man, and we who have
seen Christ, and who know something at least of the
difference Christ can make, ought to say it even more
emphatically than he, "while I live I will praise the Lord:
I will sing praises unto my God while I have any being."

The Keynote of Every Prayer

That is our function as Christians, our first duty and
our last. Are we fulfilling it? Take note of *our prayers*. Is
praise always the keynote there? Or are our prayers not
sometimes a kind of aggrieved and querulous protest to a
God who seems to manage things so badly for us? In one
or two of the earlier psalms the writer is on his knees,
saying in effect, "Now, God, just look at your universe–
look at my own unhappy miserable lot! Is this all you can
do for me, O God?"–and so on through verse after verse
of lugubrious, ungrateful self-pity; though indeed if you
read these same psalms right through you nearly always
come to a point where the man pulls himself up, as
though in a kind of sudden access of shame that makes

him blush, and then (as Paul would say) in "indignation and revenge" at himself, sweeps the low mood from his soul; and before he is finished he is crying, "Praise God from whom all blessings flow!" Never let us forget that praise is to be the keynote, the beginning, middle, and end, of every prayer.

The Keynote of Every Hymn

Or take note of *our hymns and songs*. Is praise the keynote there? Ah, sometimes to hear us Christians sing, you would hardly guess (certainly a stranger coming among us would never guess) that it is the most glorious theme in the world we are celebrating! Take some of the great Easter hymns, for instance—songs like "Jesus Christ Is Risen Today," or "The Strife Is O'er, the Battle Done." I cannot understand any one who does not want to stand up and sing these with all his heart and mind, to stand with soul on tiptoe, as it were, and with every fiber of his spiritual being in it—which is the only right way to sing; when it is the risen Christ of whom you are singing. Or take a hymn like "For All the Saints," mounting up at last to that mighty verse:

> But, lo! there breaks a yet more glorious day;
> The saints triumphant rise in bright array;
> The King of Glory passes on His way.
> Hallelujah!

Quite frankly, I cannot understand any one who, when that is being sung, does not lift up his head and put his very self into it, not with any mumbled, self-conscious, uncertain Hallelujah at the end, which may mean anything or nothing, but with a real, ringing, confident "Hallelujah!" Gairdner of Cairo one day, speaking of the "Hallelujah Chorus," exclaimed, "What an opportunity for a sanctified shout to God!" That was putting it crudely no doubt, but the root of the matter was there. The very foundations of the empire of darkness, declares one of the marching-songs of the Church, "quiver at the shout of praise." Do they, indeed? Do our Christian songs really make the principalities and powers of that dim empire tremble to hear them, as the Cavaliers trembled when Cromwell's Ironsides raised their psalms? Are we realizing that *praise is the central act of worship*, not something to be drifted through indifferently, and so on to something more important, but actually the central thing? For that is the truth. And we all have to take our share and make it central – this duty of praise to God.

The Keynote of Our Life

But even that is only touching the surface of the matter yet. For after all, it is not just a question of our prayers and hymns: it is a question of the *whole tone of our life*. Is praise the keynote there? Some people indeed are constitutionally low-set, always more conscious of the clouds than of the blue skies of life. Nearly every one passes through phases of that. Even Martin Luther, brave, high-spirited soul that he was, burst out one day, "The world's an evil fellow; let's hope God will soon end him!" We do experience these low moods when the fountains of praise and gratitude in us are all dried up. "The world's winter is going," said George Eliot on such a day, "but my everlasting winter is setting in."

The question is, How are we to avoid that, and keep a perpetually praising spirit? Well, it is partly at least a matter of right selection. I mean that when praise and gratitude wither and decay, it is because we have been concentrating on the wrong things. If a man fixes on his disadvantages and difficulties, and gazes all the time at these, it is the easiest thing in the world to get up a case against God. It is almost inevitable that he develops the "sorry scheme of things" attitude, which wants to shatter the whole plan to bits and start anew.

Praise for His Mercies, First

Hence the praising, grateful spirit is, partly at least, a matter of right selection. No man ought to start totalling up his disadvantages till he has sat down first to count his mercies. When you experience the pull of the low mood, and feel that there is a host of things against you, and that your lot is surely harder than most, then is the time to cry to your own soul, "Stop! All that may be true enough, all these hard things may be there, but before we look at that, soul of mine, you and I are going to do something else; we are going to look at the providences!" It is a Christian's duty to fix on the mercies first. And they are always there. "You call the chess-board black," says Browning's Bishop Blougram in effect, "but try looking at it from another point, and see if you don't have to call it white!" A friend in trouble once wrote to Charles Lamb that the world seemed "drained of all its sweets." To which Lamb replied, "Drained of its sweets? I don't know what you mean. Are there not roses and violets still in the earth, and the sun and moon still reigning in heaven?" The man was not looking for the providences. George Borrow's (the great Bible colporter in Spain) gypsy knew better. "In blindness," said he, "there's still the wind on the wasteland!" Once when Rainy, the great churchman, was passing through a time of public obloquy and misunderstanding, a sympathetic friend said to him that he did not know how Rainy could bear it. "Ah, but then, you see," came the quiet answer with a smile, "I'm very happy at home!" Yes, *the darkest night has stars in it*, and a Christian is a man who fixes not on the darkness but on the stars; and especially on the one bright and morning star that is always shining—Jesus! When the low mood comes, open your New Testament. Read it imaginatively. Stand on the shore at Capernaum. Visit the home at Bethany. Sit by Jacob's well, and in the upper room. Look into Jesus' eyes. Listen to His voice. Take a walk round by Calvary. Remember the crown of thorns. Then tell yourself (for it is truth), "All this was for me! The Son of God loved me, and gave Himself for me." And see if a passion of praise does not send the low mood flying, and you begin to feel like Charles Kingsley when he wrote to a friend, "Must we not thank, and thank, and thank forever, and toil and toil forever for Him?" "While I live I will praise Thee: I will sing praises to my God while I have any being."

Praise for Everything

But this question of making a right selection is not the inmost secret yet. We may train ourselves to praise by fixing on our mercies rather than on our disadvantages. But the whole lesson has not been learned till we can *praise God for everything*, the clouds as well as the sunshine, the darkness as well as the stars.

Now this I believe to be the supreme value to us of the men who wrote the psalms. They stand, these men, at every turn of the road, facing every sort of experience that can come to us, and there they cry, "Praise ye the Lord!" They stand over our sickbeds and say, "Praise ye the Lord!" They stand beside our worst disappointments and cry, "Praise ye the Lord!" They stand beside our open graves and whisper, "Praise ye the Lord!" That is faith's victory.

There is one tremendous page of Scripture on which we are shown a saint of God visited by trouble, one terrible blow after another coming down on him until his whole life was reeling; and when the bitter day that had beggared and ruined him was closing, Job, with set face and clenched hands and bent head, was sitting there, muttering something almost fiercely and desperately to himself: "The Lord gave, the Lord hath taken away" (Job 1:21). And to begin with, I imagine, he could not get beyond that, could not add another word, but only kept on repeating it in a stunned, dazed, uncertain way, "The Lord gave, and the Lord hath taken." And then there was dead silence. And for a moment everything was in the balance, his soul, his religion, his attitude to God, his very life, everything in the balance; and in the silence it was just as if the unseen world and all God's guardian angels were waiting for what would come next, wondering if it would be the soul's last cry of desolation, some dreadful anathema on life and God and heaven—waiting, wondering while he fought his battle; but then suddenly, breaking the silence, half a sob and half a shout it came, "Blessed be the name of the Lord!" Faith's victory! Praise from the depths!

Old Alan Cameron, the Covenanter, was lying a prisoner in the Tolbooth in Edinburgh, when suddenly the door of his cell burst open and in came soldiers, carrying something. "Look!" they said, uncovering it. And Alan Cameron looked. It was the head of his own boy, Richard, slain for Christ. And the old man staggered as if struck in the face with a whip. But then he lifted his head. "It is the Lord," he said, "good is the will of the Lord." Faith's victory!

Ah, now we know what the prophet meant who called not only on the flowers and trees to sing their praise to the God of hosts, but on the bare desolate ruins and dead ashes of a glory that had been humbled to the dust: "Sing together, ye waste places of Jerusalem!" For the last victory of the saints is to be able to praise God for everything—even as Jesus took the bread in token of His body and broke it, and over that broken symbol gave God thanks; took the cup, brimming over with all the bitterness of death, and gave God thanks; went out from the upper room to Gethsemane's sweat and agony, singing a hymn, and giving God thanks! It is that grateful, praising Christ who can make us sons of praise like Himself, men and women who have found the secret of a fortitude stronger than any pain, of a peace unshaken by any assaults of doubt, and of a joy that smiles through the blinding tears of defeated dreams and the bitterest disappointments that human hearts can know. It is only Jesus who can guarantee the soul's high victory. But His power to do it is unquestioned. He can make us strong, in face of everything, to praise the Lord, and to sing praises unto our God while we have any being.

Simple Duty: Praise Him

So we come back finally to this, that Christian praise is not in any sense a mere matter of inclination; it is a matter of simple duty. And it is a duty in three directions.

It is our duty to God. There was a day when Jesus on the road healed ten lepers; and one of them, finding that

that living death was really over, came running back to pour his grateful soul at Jesus' feet. "Where are the other nine?" asked Jesus. And he must be deaf indeed who does not hear in that question something like the hurt sob of the Son of God.

> Blow, blow, thou winter wind,
> Thou art not so unkind
> As man's ingratitude

to God! "Where are the nine?"

Isaiah, in a day of national apostasy, when all God's toil in His chosen vineyard seemed ending in nothing but a harvest of rank weeds, heard God crying, "What more could have been done in My vineyard than what I have done?" (Isa. 5:4). After all that—this! The Galilean pilgrims and all the friends of Jesus were shouting their Hosannas around Him as He rode into Jerusalem on the first Palm Sunday long ago, when some sour-faced people approached and advised Him to rebuke them. "I tell you," retorted Christ, "if these should hold their peace, the very stones would cry out!" And must we not say that if, after what God in Christ has done for us, delivering our eyes from tears and our feet from falling and our souls from death, if after that we are not simply throbbing with gratitude and praise, then the stones of the street and the stones of the houses where we live, and the stones of the church where we worship, might well cry out against us? Praise is our duty to God.

It is our duty to our own souls. In the story of that saintly soul who died some years ago, Francis Chavasse, Bishop of Liverpool, one favorite sentence of the Bishop's stands out as a guiding light of all his life: "Praise and service are great healers." It is worth trying to get inside the meaning of that. Praise and service are great healers. In other words, when life grows sore and wounding, and it is difficult to be brave, praise God; and if it is hard to do it, make yourself do it, and in the very act of praise the wound will begin to heal. Sing something, and you will rally your own heart with the song! Praise and service are great healers. Praise brings the wounded back to life's firing-line again. And thus praise is our duty to our own souls.

It is our duty to our brother man. For Christian praise has this property about it—that it is contagious. One song begets another, and the spark of praise leaps from heart to heart. One man with praise to God in his soul will start others singing who would never have thought of raising the song themselves. It is said of that great missionary-soldier of Jesus, Francis Xavier, by one of his own contemporaries, that if ever any of the brothers were sad, the way they took to be happy was just to go and look at him. That is how your praise can help. It is a troubled, tangled world in which we are living now; and God knows there is enough darkness in it without our doing anything, by dulness or depression or sullen cynicism, to make that darkness deeper. The real servant of humanity today is the man whose life breathes praise. Keep sounding that note, and even when you do not know it, others will be facing life more valiantly because of you, and they may be thanking God that you were born.

Spiritual Worship

Frederick W. Robertson (1816–1853) wanted to be a soldier, but he yielded to his father's decision that he take orders in the Anglican church. The courage that he would have shown on the battlefield, he displayed in the pulpit, where he fearlessly declared truth as he saw it. Never strong physically, he experienced deep depression, he questioned his faith, and he often wondered if his ministry was doing any good. He died a young man, in great pain, but in great faith and courage. He had ministered for only six years at Trinity Chapel, Brighton, but today his printed sermons have taken his brave message around the world. These two combined sermons are from his *Sermons, Fifth Series*, published in 1900 in London by Kegan Paul, Trench, Trübner and Company. Each one is but a "skeleton" summary, yet each contains more truth than some complete sermons by others!

Frederick W. Robertson

7

SPIRITUAL WORSHIP

Jesus saith unto her, Woman, believe me, the hour cometh, when ye shall neither in this mountain, nor yet at Jerusalem, worship the Father. Ye worship ye know not what: we know what we worship: for salvation is of the Jews. But the hour cometh, and now is, when the true worshipers shall worship the Father, in spirit and in truth: for the Father seeketh such to worship him. God is a Spirit: and they that worship him must worship him in spirit and in truth (John 4:21–24).

CHRIST RESTS on the narrow rocky road between Gerizim and Ebal, before entering Sychar, near a well. A Samaritan woman comes to draw water. He asks for a drink. There had been a long controversy between the Jews and Samaritans as to the whereabouts of worship; and this turned on an antiquarian point as to which was the correct reading in Deuteronomy 27. Hence arose theological rancor. The Jews had no dealings with the Samaritans except in traffic and business; no giving or asking kindness. The woman, brought up in this system of malignity, marvels at Christ putting Himself under an obligation to her, a Samaritan.

In the conversation that ensued Christ's uncommon character appeared to her. Instantly, thinking the time had come for the solution of the controversy, she puts the question, partly to escape from a conversation which was becoming too personal, partly from that love of controversy which is so common in all of us. But Christ had no intention that it should end so. Hence, He takes the opportunity to define spiritual worship.

Our subject divides itself into:

1.) Errors which interfered with purity of religious worship, and 2.) the nature of the worship which God accepts.

Errors Which Interfered With
Purity of Religious Worship

The first error *arises from a tendency to localize God.* Her question was, in fact, "Where?" Christ's reply was, "Nowhere in particular – everywhere."

This question lies at the root of all superstition. It is observable among the heathen, who confine the agency of a god to a certain district: among the uneducated poor of our country, in their notions of a cemetery; and among the more refined, in the mysterious idea which they attach to a church, an altar, and the elements of the sacrament.

Let us define what we mean by sanctity of place. It is a thing merely subjective, not objective; it is relative to us. It belongs to that law of association by which a train of ideas returns more easily by suggestion in some one place than in another. Worship in a festive room, or over a shop, would suggest notions uncongenial with devotion. Hence, the use of *setting apart*, or consecrating places for worship. There is no other sanctity of place. Transfer what is in you to the place and you verge on superstition. Therefore the church, the altar, etc., are not holy – God is not there.

We hear an objection to this. It is said to be dangerous to say this: it will unsettle people's minds, a little of this illusion is wholesome, especially for the poor. To this reply, in the first place, Christ did not so reason. Consider how unsettling this was to the woman. The little religion she had clung to Mount Gerizim. The shock of being told that it was not holy might have unsettled all her religion. Did Christ hesitate one moment? And, in the second place, we are only concerned with truth. Some people are afraid of truth. As if God's truth could be dangerous! The straight road is ever the nearest. People *must* bear, and shall, what an earnest mind dares to say. Is God there or not? If not, at our peril we say He is.

The holiest place! Is this church holy? Yes, if a holy congregation is in it; if not, it is brick and mortar. Which is the holiest place in it? The altar? Nay; the spirit of the holiest man present. Which is the holiest place on earth?

Not where architecture, music, solemn aisles, or fretted roof, yield their spell; but perhaps a wretched pallet on which one of Christ's humblest ones is dying, or a square foot of ground on which a heroic Christian stands.

A second error *arises from the idea that forms are immutable.* "Our fathers worshiped in this mountain," therefore we must.

Let me explain what a form is. It is the shape in which an age expresses a feeling. The spirit of religion remains, but the expression alters.

There is, for instance, the present love of antiquity. Let us do it justice. Enthusiasm is lovely – it is far better than coolness; but is it right?

There is a wish to restore the observances and the rubrics of the early Church. I will try to show why it is now not necessary. The times are altered. Religion is domestic now, then it was social . . . Public daily prayer would be a mistake now. . . .

A third error *arises from ignorance:* "Ye worship ye know not what."

There is a feeling of devoutness inherent in the human mind. We hear the solemn tones of a child when repeating his prayer or hymns. Before what is greater, wiser, better than himself, man bows instinctively. But the question is, *what* will he worship? We distinguish, therefore, between instinctive devoutness and enlightened worship.

To many there are three deities – Power, Wisdom, and Goodness.

The heathen bend before Power. The Universe was alive with deity to him: he saw God in the whirlwind, the lightning, and the thunder. This is ignorance.

The philosopher is above this. He bows before Wisdom. Science tells him of electricity, gravitation, force. He looks down on warm devoutness; for he sees only contrivance and mind in Nature. He admires all calmly, without enthusiasm. He calls it Rational religion. This also is ignorance.

The spiritual man bows before Goodness, "The true worshipers worship the Father" "We know what we worship: for salvation is of the Jews," that is, God is intelligible in Christ as Love, Goodness, and Purity. None but this is intelligent worship.

A fourth error *is a mistake about the nature of reverence.*

To have no veneration is to have no religion. But let me explain what reverence is. This Samaritan woman had what they call reverence, veneration for antiquity, zeal for her church, lingering recollections of the old mountain, respect for a prophet. But what was her life? He with whom she then lived was not her husband. In other words, reverence, veneration, awe, are a class of feelings which belong to the imagination and are neither good nor bad: they may go along with religion, but also they may not. A man may kneel to sublime things, yet never have bent his heart to goodness and purity. A man may be reverential, and yet impure.

Next examine a man who is called irreverent. Constitutionally so framed that he does not happen to thrill at painted windows, Gothic architecture and solemn music; is he, therefore, without veneration? Take him out into God's grand universe, or put before him Christ's character; is there no adoration, no deep, intense love? Tell him of a self-denying action; is there no moisture in his eye? Tempt him to meanness; is there no indignant scorn? The man has bowed his soul before Justice, Mercy, Truth, and therefore stands erect before everything else which this world calls sublime.

True Character of Spiritual Worship

1. It *consists in a right appreciation of God's character.* Here it is presented in a twofold aspect: "God is a *Spirit;*" and "the true worshipers shall worship the *Father.*"

What is meant by spirit? There are false notions which

regard it as attenuated gas, a wreath of air or vapor. Observe, this is only subtle materialism.

Consider the universe, with the sun and stars, the harmony of the planets. All this force, order, harmony — that is God. The Spring season, with bursting vegetation — its life is God. Our own minds, their thought and feeling — that is spirit. God, therefore, is the *Mind* of the universe. Force, law, harmony — all this is God. And yet notice the coldness of this, for He is thus revealed only as a God for the intellect, not for the heart.

Therefore, for the heart He is revealed as a *Father*. Consider the endearing meaning of this word — in it tenderness is united with reverence. Let us fasten on one meaning out of many. Let us take the work of a father in education. Consider the use of this rugged, stubborn, material world to invigorate the mind by trying it against difficulties. Agriculture, steam navigation, are the result. Consider the use of suffering. The cross is the emblem of life. It is only through struggle, through difficulty, that the soul can be invigorated. All that is a Fatherly work. Who would wish to have his child luxurious, rich, indolent, rather than see him in honest poverty, struggling with sorrow? This explains what would otherwise be this "unintelligible world." We can take the bitter draught thankfully. "The cup which my Father hath given me, shall I not drink it?" (John 18:11).

Nature of Worship Which God Accepts

2. Next, spiritual worship *consists in spiritual character*. The true worshipers are those who "worship the Father in spirit and in truth."

That is, holy character is a kind of worship. All true life is worship: "Worship the Lord in the beauty of holiness;" "Lo, I come to do thy will, O Lord." Before a material God a material knee would have to bow. Before a spiritual God, nothing but the prostration of the spirit can be acceptable.

> He prayeth well, who loveth well
> Both man and bird and beast.

Love is a kind of prayer — the truest lifting up of the soul.

And Now the Application

1. Christ came to bring man's spirit into immediate contact with God's Spirit; to sweep away everything intermediate. In lonely union, face to face, man's spirit and God's Spirit must come together. It is a grand thought! Aspire to this! Aspire to greatness, goodness! So let your spirit mingle with the spirit of the Everlasting.

2. Scripture insists on *truth* of character. God is made known as a real God. The worshiper is to be a real character. The Christian must be a true man—transparent, who can bear to be looked through and through. There must be no pretense; no gilded tinsel—TRUE GOLD ALL THROUGH.

TRUE WORSHIPERS

The conversation between Christ and the woman of Samaria began on common topics. By and by it became more deep and interesting. He, to whom all things here were types, could not converse without a Divine meaning in all He said. A drink of water connected itself with the mystery of life. So soon as she discovered His spiritual character she put the question of her day.

A miserable question had perplexed two nations lying near each other, of the same blood, interests, and hopes. They hated each other: "the Jew had no dealing with the Samaritan." They excommunicated each other. Just in proportion to their nearness of relationship was their bitterness. A Jew hated a Samaritan far more than a heathen. Scarcely anything in the present day will exactly illustrate this hatred. For the spirit of men is the same in every age. And the intensity of abhorrence between Jew and Samaritan was the measure of their zeal. The more they kept aloof from their "brother whom they had seen," the more they thought they showed their love to "God, whom they had *not* seen."

Two Introductory Thoughts

Before we consider our subject we have two remarks to make.

Notice, first, *the difference between interest in theology and interest in religion.* Here was a woman living in sin, and yet deeply interested in a religious controversy. She found, doubtless, a kind of safeguard to rest on in the perception of this keen interest. Her religion was almost nothing, her theology most orthodox.

Theological controversy sharpens our disputative faculties and awakens our speculative ones. Religion is love to God and man. People do not distinguish between theology and religion. They make skill in controversy a test of spirituality; yet it is but a poor test. However, this is the test we use. The way the woman questioned Christ is a specimen of a common feeling. The moment Christ appears she examines His views. She does not ask whether the Man before her were pure and spotless – His life spent in doing good; but was He sound upon the vital question of the temple?

A man dies and you ask what were his opinions. Consider which is worse – a mistake about baptism or a mistake about love to God and man? The *life* is the test of faith.

The second remark we make is, that *all that was worth notice in the question had disappeared.*

Formally the Jew was right, the Samaritan wrong: "Jerusalem was the place where men ought to worship."

But wrong as the Samaritan was, he was not half so wrong for praying on Mount Gerizim as the Jew was for excommunicating him and having no dealings with him: or half so wrong as he was himself for hating the Jew. "And they did not receive him, because his face was as though he would go to Jerusalem" (Luke 9:53). Right as was the Jew in his theology, it was negated by his hatred of the Samaritan. The duty of being liberal to the illiberal was forgotten. And thus, worship had disappeared in disputes about the place "where men ought to worship."

This belongs to us: we too have our miserable questions of *where?* and *when?* Every age has its own special question. The question once was, whether a miracle was performed in the Communion. The questions now are whether a miracle is performed in the baptism of a baby; whether rule resides in the state or in the church; whether the priest is above the law or beneath it.

The days are coming when these questions will be debated with vehemence; and in proportion to our controversial staunchness we shall estimate our spiritual excellence. And the days perhaps are coming when we shall test each other by these questions, and pronounce all who disagree with us bad men, and refuse communion with them.

Yet, observe, while we battle about baptism—how and in what sense it makes us children of God, literally or figuratively—we are losing all that baptism means. Instead of a symbol of unity, "one baptism," it becomes ingeniously converted into a symbol of strife.

Just as worship disappeared in the miserable controversy about "the place where men ought to worship," Mount Gerizim or Mount Moriah, so is Christianity slipping while we battle about baptism—when, and where, the Spirit of God comes down.

Now tell us which was worse—to worship on a wrong hill, or to mistake the very essence of worship? Which was worse—to err respecting the interpretation of records on which the question rested *where* God had placed His name, or to err respecting love? A blunder of intellect, or a lack of charity? Which is worse—to hold incorrect views respecting baptism, or to lose the whole of that for which baptism was given?—to sacrifice before a wrong altar, or to bring wrong sacrifice to a true altar?

Now Christ speaks of a new worship essentially different from the old. He made religion spiritual, He pointed out the difference between religion and theology, and He revealed the foundation on which true worship must rest.

A new time was coming for a new worship: "The hour cometh and now is, when the true worshipers shall worship the Father in spirit and in truth."

Let us consider: 1.) The foundation, on which the new worship rests, and 2.) the nature of spiritual worship.

The Foundation of Spiritual Worship

The foundation on which the new worship rests is a revelation made by Christ respecting the character of God, which contains three points: His paternity, "God is the Father;" His spiritual nature, "God is a Spirit;" and His personality, "He seeketh."

1. *God is "the Father."* This is evidently the emphatic word of the sentence: "The hour cometh, and now is, when the true worshipers shall worship the *Father*."

Christ revealed a name: the Father. Great stress is laid in the Bible upon the significance of names. Moses asked, "What is thy name?"—"I am that I am, I appeared to the fathers by the name of God Almighty, but by my name Jehovah was I not known to them." This was of peculiar importance in Jewish theology. A name was identical with the person; Moses means drawn out of the water; Jacob, supplanter; Israel, Prince of God. So each step in revelation added something to the name, first God, then Jehovah expressing His Being, lastly Holy Father, revealing His Character.

Note however, that men had in a sense before worshiped a father. The Greeks and the Romans spoke of the "father of gods and men." The Jewish prophets said, "Have we not all one father?" But the universality in the Name was wanting. A Father—yes, but of Rome alone, or Athens alone, or the Jews alone.

Therefore, the old question was all in all. *Where* is He to be worshiped? For the real question hidden under that was, *Who* are His children? For if God be localized to one place, then His children are those alone who worship there. Is it the Capitoline Jove, or the Zeus of Olympus, or Jehovah of Mount Zion, or the Father of the family of man who is to be worshiped?

The appearance of Christ was the manifestation of the answer: God is the Father of the family of man. The incarnation declared that the Son of Man is the Son of God. One appeared who was not the Jew, nor the Greek, nor the Roman, but the Man; One in whose veins ran the blood of the human race; One in whose character was neither exclusively the woman nor the man, but all that was most manly, and all that was most womanly – One so tender to the publican and to the sinner that He could say to Mary Magdalene, "My Father and your Father."

All are born sons of God into this world. Yet make no mistake. There is a distinction between a son of God by right and a son of God in fact. The last century beheld the son of a royal house taken from his family and compelled to descend into the lowest ranks of life. He was heir of the royal family; by right, heir to the throne, but in fact, heir to degradation – vile in character, ignorant, and unregal. So is it with the son of man. By right, a child of God; by fact, a child of wrath, ignorant of his privileges, not knowing who or what he is, or "that imperial palace whence he came."

2. *The second foundation on which spiritual worship rests, is that "God is a Spirit."*

We should greatly mistake the meaning of this if we took it as a theological definition of the being of God. It is not theological, but practical. It is chiefly negative. It says what God is not: He is not matter, He has not a form. "A spirit hath not flesh and bones." He is Mind. Mind, properly speaking, has no *place*. Of love, generosity, thought – can you say *when?*

This, then, was the great truth, that God is a Mind, not separated by conditions of space and time from His creatures.

3. *The third foundation on which spiritual worship rests is the Personality of God:* "The Father seeketh."

There are two erroneous notions, both compatible with the idea of Spirit, that God is an idea elaborated out of our own minds, and that God is the soul of Nature. There is a prevalent notion that God is an idea elaborated out of our own minds; we have an idea of justice, truth, mercy; and this idea or assemblage of ideas we insensibly invest with personality and call it God. Notions of this sort more or less float in all our minds, haunting us so that we lose the idea of personality. And then spiritual worship would be only this, cultivating goodness, cultivating truth, cultivating justice.

The other prevalent notion is that God is the Soul of Nature, the Spirit of the Universe. But at once you feel this is not religion. Oh, no! that utter loneliness of soul which comes from sin and despair, needs some one near on whom to lean, some one who can feel and sympathize. One *is* near and feels. No Soul of Nature, no abstract goodness, no ideal of our own minds, no Spirit of the Universe. Not an unconscious mind becoming broken into a myriad consciousnesses; but a living Father who "seeketh."

This is Redemption. This is the doctrine of Holy Spirit: "God is a Spirit – He seeketh."

Oh, if in this dreary life, when one is struggling for truth, and struggling to God alone, it is only that we are realizing the ideal of our own minds!

Here is the value of belief in a Person. Personality belongs to spirit; not less personal because spirit. And, therefore, our Redeemer tells us this truth, "the Father seeketh such to worship Him," – not that we seek God, but that He seeks us; not that we rise to God, but that He descends to us.

This it is upon which we base our conviction that there will be hereafter a spiritual worship. But when we are told that the Creator has interested Himself in His creation, we know that the day shall come when the "true worshipers shall worship the Father in spirit and in truth."

The Nature of Spiritual Worship

Now what we mean by "worship" is the highest reverence of the soul; adoration, awe; it may be, even, vague devoutness: "Ye know not what."

There is a vast difference between a man's creed and

his worship. It is not merely what a man *professes* to reverence that constitutes worship. Moreover, to be spiritual, worship must be intelligent. It must be higher than mere words. It is possible for a Trinitarian to call Christ God, and worship mammon. It is conceivable that an Unitarian theologian may in word—I say conceivable—deny even the Deity of Christ, and yet, like the son in the parable who said, "I go," and went not, that he may have learned to give Him the whole reverence of his soul: "Not every one that saith unto Me, Lord, Lord, shall enter into the kingdom of heaven, but he that doeth the will of my Father which is in heaven" (Matt. 7:21).

Again, it is not a thing which a man can decide, whether he will be a worshiper or not, a worshiper he *must* be, the only question is *what* will he worship? Every man worships—is a born worshiper. It is nonsense to say he does not believe in a God. Before what is greater than himself man bows instinctively. The feeling of devoutness is instinctive. Look at the child when he first enters the church of God, how his soul seems filled with the grandeur of the service, how he tries to join his voice with the praises that are being uttered. It is man's necessity that he must love. He may call himself an infidel if he will, but he must worship something; it may be perchance himself, or the rights of man, or even reason.

1. The new worship of God is to be a *universal worship:* "Neither in this mountain nor yet at Jerusalem shall men worship the Father" (John 4:21). Are we then to understand by this that the difference between the old and the new worship is merely that the one is localized and the other not? [Observe there was a use of space and place before the Father was known. Zeus of Olympus and Jove of the Capitol compared in effects.] Nay, the distinction is not that; what is meant here is that it is not in Mount Moriah or Mount Gerizim only, but everywhere that we are to worship the Father. The distinction is between exclusive and universal worship. The time was coming when the question *where* would be unimportant.

A mistake is sometimes made that local worship is here forbidden, that worship in a place is not spiritual worship, and that we must go into the temple of nature to worship the Father in spirit. We are told that the everlasting hills are pillars far more grand than the pillars of the church, and that the sky above is far more glorious than the roof of the most splendid cathedral. But there is in the worship in the temple of nature something elevating and grand; we feel ourselves higher than the nature we contemplate, and so our pride begins to rise, and when we come back from it to worship among men, we find that we had been forgetting humanity, and the family of spirits congenial to us. Therefore, do not fly to nature for spiritual worship. We must content ourselves with a worship far less grand, but quite as true, and more humble.

2. Again, the new worship of God must be *worship "in spirit."*

This truth the better men among the Jews had gradually seen. The later prophets had clearer and higher notions of worship than their predecessors. This we see from their notion of sacrifice: "Lo, I come to do thy will, O Lord," and, again, "He hath shown thee, O man, what is good; and what doth the Lord require of thee, but to do justice, to love mercy, and to walk humbly with thy God" (Mic. 6:8). They recognized that all true life is worship: "Worship the Lord in the beauty of holiness."

3. Lastly, this spiritual worship consists in *worship in truth* . . . When we are told to worship the Lord in truth, it means the correspondence between acts and laws. . . . In spiritual life there are certain laws, obedience to which is truest worship. God dwells in the humble and contrite heart; to fear God, to be humble, and to love God, that is the spiritual worship of God.

Self-denial, an Element of Worship

George H. Morrison (1866–1928) assisted the great
Alexander Whyte in Edinburgh, pastored two churches,
and then became pastor in 1902 of the distinguished
Wellington Church on University Avenue in Glasgow.
His preaching drew great crowds; in fact, people had to
queue up an hour before the services to be sure to get
seats in the large auditorium. Morrison is a master of
imagination in preaching, yet his messages are solidly
biblical. From his many published volumes of sermons,
I have chosen this message, found in *The Return of the
Angels*, published in 1909 by Hodder and Stoughton,
London.

George H. Morrison

8

SELF-DENIAL,
AN ELEMENT OF WORSHIP

Bring an offering, and come into His courts (Psalm 96:8).

IN PUBLIC WORSHIP in the sanctuary there are certain demands made of every worshiper. There are certain elements which must be present, if the worship is to be in spirit and in truth. There is, for instance, the element of *thanksgiving* for the goodness of God to us from day to day. There is the sense of *spiritual need,* and the knowledge that none but God can meet that need. There is the sense of *indebtedness* to Christ who loved us and gave Himself for us; in whose death there is our only hope, and in whose Spirit is our only strength. All these elements must meet and mingle if our worship is to be worship in reality. Without them, a man shall come to church, and go from it no better than he came. But there is another element, not less important, yet one which is very frequently ignored, and that is the element of *self-sacrifice*. We all know that worship calls for praise. We must remember it also calls for self-denial. There are many to whom worship is a joy; but it is more than a joy, it is a duty. And it is a duty, when we conceive it rightly, of such a lofty and supersensual nature, that to perform it rightly is impossible, save in a certain measure of self-sacrifice. On that thought, then, I am going to dwell—on the element of sacrifice in worship. I want to impress upon you that to worship God must always make demands on self-denial. And my prayer is, that so considering the matter, our common worship may become a nobler thing, and we may escape that lightness in regarding it which is so prevalent and so pernicious.

Giving in Worship

To begin with, that element of sacrifice is seen in the matter of the money-offering. "Bring an offering, and come into His courts." No Jew came to his worship empty-handed. To give of his means was part of his devotions. Of the thirteen boxes in the Temple treasury, four were for the free-will offerings of the people. And this fine spirit of the ancient worship passed over into the worship of the Church, and was enormously deepened and intensified by the new thought of the sacrifice of Christ. "Thanks be unto God for His unspeakable gift"—that was the mainspring of Christian liberality. It was the glowing thought of all that Christ had given, which quickened the poorest to be givers too. And that so sanctified the Christian offertory that Paul can speak of the resurrection triumph, and then, as if unconscious of descent, can add "now as concerning the collection."

Now while all such offerings were acceptable to God, and while all brought a blessing to the giver, yet from earliest times it was felt by spiritual men that true giving must touch on self-denial. You remember the abhorrence of King David against offering to God that which had cost him nothing (2 Sam. 24:24). It is such touches amid all his failures that reveal the Godward genius of the king. And we have read of Jesus Christ, and of His judgment upon the widow's mite, and of all the riches that He found in that, because there was self-denial in the giving. It was a wonderful cry that broke from Zacchaeus' lips when he came face to face with Jesus Christ. "Lord," he cried, looking upon Jesus, "Lord, I give half of my goods to feed the poor" (Luke 19:8). He had always given, in his Jewish way. He had never entered the Temple without giving; but now, under the gaze of Jesus, he felt that he could not give enough. Brethren, that is the mark of Christian giving. It reaches over into self-denial. You may give as a citizen and never feel it, but I do not think you can give as a Christian so. I do not think we give in the spirit of Jesus until like Him we touch on self-denial, until His love constrains us to some sacrifice, as it constrained Him to the sacrifice of all. Let us then seriously ask ourselves: Have we been giving to the point of sacrifice? Have we ever denied ourselves anything, that we might bring an offering and come into His courts? It is only thus that giving is a joy—only thus it bring us nearer to Christ—only thus it is a means of grace, as spiritual and as strengthening as prayer.

Thus far, then, upon the very surface, but now we shall go a little deeper. For, gradually, as men became more spiritual the thought of self-denial deepened also. It was not enough, if one were to worship God, that he should bring an offering in his hand. Slowly it was borne in upon the Jew that the *truest offering was in the heart.* And nothing is more instructive in the Scriptures than to watch the development of that idea—the gradual deepening of self-sacrifice as an element in acceptable worship.

Think first of the case of David, a man who had been trained in ritual worship. You may depend upon it that from his earliest years he had never worshiped with that which cost him nothing. He had brought his offering, and he had paid for it, and he had denied himself something so that he might pay for it. The God whom he had found when he was shepherding was not a God to be worshiped on the cheap. And then there came his kingship and his fall, and the terrible havoc of his kingly character, and David found that all the blood of goats could not make him a true worshiper again. The sacrifices of God are a broken spirit; a broken and a contrite heart. Let him give his kingdom for an offering, and he would not be an acceptable worshiper. He must give himself; he must deny his lusts; he must lay aside his pride and be a penitent, or all his worship would be mockery, and the sanctuary a barren place for him. He knew from the first that worship meant denial. It was his thought of denial that was deepened. He found there was no blessing in the sanctuary unless his heart was penitent and humble. And that was a mighty truth for him to grasp, and it has enriched the worship of the ages, and has passed into the newer covenant, and into all the gatherings of its saints.

The Attitude of the Heart in Worship

Now turn to David's greater Son, and listen to the *words of Christ Himself.* He is speaking in the Sermon on the Mount, about bringing the offering to the altar: "Therefore, if thou bring thy gift to the altar, and there rememberest that thy brother hath aught against thee, leave there thy gift before the altar and go thy way. First be reconciled to thy brother and then come and offer thy gift" (Matt. 5:23, 24). *Now mark that Jesus is talking about worship.* His theme is not the patching up of quarrels. He is teaching us what elements are needed if we are to worship God in spirit and in truth.

And not only does He insist on giving—He takes that, we may say, for granted—but He insists that at the back of every gift there shall be the self-denial of the heart. It is far easier to give up a coin than it is to give up a quarrel. It is easier to lay down a generous offering than to lay down a long-continued grudge. And what Jesus Christ insists upon is this—that if worship is to be acceptable to God, the worshiper must lay aside his pride, and humble himself as a little child. That is not easy—it never can be easy. That is far from natural to man. That is hard to do, and very bitter, and quite opposed to natural inclination. And it calls for patience, and interior sacrifice, and prayerful if secret self-denial; and only thus, according to the Master, can one hope to be an acceptable worshiper. Who, then, is sufficient for these things? That is just what I want to impress upon you. I want to teach you that worship is not easy. I want to teach you that it is very hard. It is not a comfortable hour on Sunday with beautiful music and a fluent preacher. It is *an attitude of heart and soul that is impossible without self-denial.* I thank God that in the purest worship there is but little demand upon the intellect. The humblest saint, who cannot write a letter, may experience all the blessing of the sanctuary. But there *is* a demand upon the soul; there *is* a call to sacrifice and cross-bearing. For the road to church is like the road to heaven—it lies past the shadow of the cross.

Gathering Together for Worship

Well, now, to come a little nearer home, consider *our gathering to public worship*. In the very coming to church every Sunday, there must be an element of self-denial. In country places it may be different, for in country places life is often lonely. And men, in virtue of their social instinct, are glad for the weekly gathering in the church. But in the city there is always company, and the difficulty rather is to get alone; so in the city there is no social instinct to reinforce the call to public prayer. Were a man just to consult his inclination, it is probable that he would seldom come to church. And he is tired when the week is over, and is not Sunday a day of rest? And perhaps he is not feeling well, and the morning looks as if there might be rain. Not only so, but he tells you seriously that he gets more good at home than in church. And if he wants a sermon he has them on his shelves, written by the great masters of the heart, and reaching him as he is never reached by anything he hears from his own pulpit. All that may be the flimsiest excuse, or all that may be literally true. But in either case what it reveals is this, that natural inclination is not church-ward. And making all allowance for old habit, and a certain lingering of social pressure, the fact remains that self-denial is needed if one is to be every Sunday in the sanctuary.

The point is that that very self-denial is good for man and pleasing to God. It is the best of all beginnings to the week just to crush a little our easy inclinations. To do on Sunday what is our Christian duty, and doing it, to bring our will into subjection, is a better augury for a bright week than the finest sermon in the easy chair. "Then Jesus as His custom was, went into the synagogue" (Luke 4:16). Did you ever meditate upon these words? He was the Son, and heaven was His home, and yet as His custom was, He went to church. He never said, "I do not need to go—I can have fellowship with God at home." He took up His cross and He denied Himself, and He has told us to follow in His steps.

Fellowship in Worship

Pass now from the approach to worship to worship itself, and think of this first—that worship is fellowship. In public worship we are not simply hearers; we are a fellowship of Christian people. You go to a lecture just to hear the lecturer, or you go to the theater just to see a play. It does not matter who is there beside you. They are nothing to you and you are nothing to them. Not one of them would do anything for you, or seek to help you if you were in difficulty, or go to visit you if you were sick, or try to cheer you in the evil day. At the theater you have an audience; but you have not an audience in the church. You may call it so, but it is not really so, in any sanctuary that is blessed. It is a fellowship of men and women, bound together by their common faith, united by the very deepest things, and loving one another in Christ Jesus. In every fellowship must there not be a certain element of sacrifice? Is it not so in the fellowship of home, if home is to be other than a mockery? In all communion there must be self-denial, and a constant willingness to yield a little. If that be so in the fellowship of home, it must also be so in the fellowship of worship.

Just as a mother, worthy of the name, loves to deny herself for her dear children; just as a husband will regard his wife in every choice he makes, and every plan; so in the fellowship of public worship there must be mutual consideration, a constant willingness to forgo a little, for the sake of others for whom Christ has died. The young have their rights, but they will not insist on them, when they know it would vex and irritate the old. The old have their claims, but for the sake of the young, they will welcome what may not appeal to them. And when a hymn is sung, or when a word is preached, that seems to have no message for one worshiper, that worshiper will always bear in mind that for some one else that is the word in season. All that is of the essence of true worship, and all that calls for a little sacrifice. A happy home is impossible without it and also a happy congregation. A tender regard for others by our side, with the denial that is involved in that, is an integral part of public worship.

Our Approach to God in Worship

The same truth is still more evident when we think of worship as our approach to God. Worship is our approach to God by the new and living way of Jesus Christ. Now, it is true that we were made for God, and that in Him we live and move and have our being. It is true that as we awaken and as we sleep, He is not far away from any one of us. Yet such is the immersion in the world, even of the most prayerful and most watchful, that the approach to God with the whole heart demands a real effort.

Of course, you may come to church, and be in church, and never know the reality of worship. For you may think your thoughts, and dream your dreams, and be in the spirit a thousand miles away. But quietly to reject intruding thoughts, and give oneself to prayer, praise and reading, that is a task that never can be easy, and for some it is incredibly hard. If there were anything to rivet the attention, that would make all the difference in the world. In a theater, you can forget yourself, absorbed in the excitement of the play. But the church of the living God is not a theater, and in the day when it becomes theatrical, in that day its worship will be gone, with all the blessings. If you want to wander, you can always wander. There is nothing here to rivet the attention. There are only a few hymns, and a quiet prayer, and the simple reading of a page of the Scriptures. And it is for *you* to make the needed effort, and to shut the gates and to withdraw yourself, and through that very effort comes the blessedness of the public worship of God in Jesus Christ. It is thus that worship becomes a heavenly feast—when we bring our will to it and take it nobly. It is thus that worship becomes a means of grace, in a hard-driven and exciting city. Make it as attractive as you please, but remember, if it is to be blessed to you, you must deny yourself, you must take up your cross, you must bring an offering and come into His courts.

Worship . . . Delight Supreme

Walter H. Werner (1893–1987) received his biblical
training at Wesleyan College, Missouri, in preparation
for a long, fruitful ministry. He pastored churches for
thirty years and also founded Topeka Bible Church, a
strong center for evangelical outreach. His emphasis
broadened to a specialization in children's ministry. He
was appointed Kansas State Director for Child
Evangelism Fellowship and later served for many years
as Central Regional Director. Known as a true "prayer
warrior," his extensive speaking and writing ministry
includes numerous magazine articles and over two
hundred tracts. This sermon, "Worship . . . Delight
Supreme," is from *Child Evangelism* Magazine,
November, 1964.

Walter H. Werner

9

WORSHIP . . . DELIGHT SUPREME

WHEN A MAN'S HEART is right toward God and he is in unbroken fellowship with Him, in Christ, four imperatives, if followed persistently, will assure for him God's greatest pleasure in him. They may be stated simply in these four words: Praise–Prayer–Perception–Performance. Or stated in a little rhyme they may appear like this: Worship–Pray–Listen–Obey.

We find these four imperatives clearly and simply set before us in the record of the meeting of Joshua with the Captain of the Lord's host on the plain of Jericho. Let us take a look at it in Joshua 5:13–15.

"And it came to pass, when Joshua was by Jericho, that he lifted up his eyes and looked, and, behold, there stood a man over against him with his sword drawn in his hand: and Joshua went unto him, and said unto him, Art thou for us or for our adversaries? And he said, Nay; but as captain of the host of the LORD am I now come. And Joshua fell on his face to the earth, and did worship, and said unto him, What saith my lord unto his servant? And the captain of the LORD'S host said unto Joshua, Loose thy shoe from off thy foot; for the place whereon thou standest is holy. And Joshua did so."

Let us observe, in rapid succession, the four imperatives mentioned above. First comes worship, or praise (v. 14, ". . . and did worship. . ."). Next comes prayer (v. 14, "What saith my lord unto his servant?"). Then follows listening, or perception (v. 15, "Loose thy shoe from off thy foot. . ."). And then follows obedience, or performance (v. 15, "And Joshua did so."). These four imperatives are so inclusive in the life of each of us, that if accepted and carried out, they will fill our lives with God Himself and bring us to our continual highest usefulness in His hands.

These four imperatives constitute the Christian's response to God's claim upon his life. We are God's creatures by physical birth and His new creatures by spiritual birth. All life, physical and spiritual, is a gift from His hand. So also is the maintenance of life. He has created us and sustains us for the sole purpose of bringing glory to Him. We have no other reason for existing. In bringing glory to His name, we become participants of His glory. Why shouldn't He present His claim, and why shouldn't we respond, gladly, willingly, completely?

It is the purpose of the rest of this message to consider the first of these imperatives, namely *worship*. This is, by the very nature of the subject, inexhaustible. So let us simply look at it in these five essentials: (1) What is worship? (2) Preparation for worship, (3) How to worship, (4) Classes of worshipers, and (5) Results of worship.

What Is Worship?

Worship is not easily defined. It is so interwoven with prayer and Bible study that it is not easy to tell where worship ends and prayer and Bible study begin. It must not be imagined that since there are these four imperatives in the believer's life, that each must or can be kept in a compartment of its own. Worship may take place again and again in the midst of prayer, of Bible study, and of simple child-like obedience. Yet at the heart or essence, each of these four imperatives is distinct from the other three.

In worship, for instance, we bring something to the Lord; in prayer, we come to ask and receive something of the Lord; in listening, we read God's Word and learn His instructions and will; and in obeying, we do what He commands. Worship is not prayer, not Bible study, nor obedience in commission. These are rather the outflow of worship. Joshua prayed, he listened, and he obeyed because he first worshiped. Worship prepares the heart and makes prayer, Bible study, and obedience a great privilege and joy, a real delight instead of a duty.

Worship is estimating God aright, putting Him in His proper place, where He is ALL to us, and putting ourselves in our proper place, where we are nothing in ourselves. When God is ALL, there is no room for others or for self. As Joshua worshiped the Captain of the Lord's host, he himself was leveled to the ground, nothing.

When David worshiped, he lost sight of all else and cried out, "Whom have I in heaven but thee? and there is none upon earth that I desire besides thee" (Ps. 73:25). When Paul worshiped he said, "For to me to live is Christ, and to die is gain" (Phil. 1:21).

Worship is in process when we adore our God, when we admire, exalt, and honor Him. It is done in truth and in Spirit, as we whisper or shout or sing our praises to Him, all others excluded. It is doing private business with our Savior and Lord, in secret, as we love Him freely as He loves us. Only those who so worship the Lord, in secret, alone with Him, do ever worship Him in public. But as they do so daily in secret, it is bound to break out on them in public and in the congregation.

Preparation for Worship

Preparation for true worship is the work of the Lord in our hearts. Our business is to yield to Him. In Philippians 2:13, we read, ". . . it is God which worketh in you both to will and to do of his good pleasure." All the work of godly living, at the top of which stands worship, is entirely outside of our natural ability. For by nature we are dead in trespasses and sins. Jeremiah says "The heart is deceitful above all things, and desperately wicked" (Jer. 17:9). Can worship of a holy God flow out of a heart like that? Let us observe four things among the most elementary requirements for worship.

1. *Regeneration*

It goes almost without saying, yet God's Word is most explicit on this point, that the spiritually dead soul of the natural man must be made alive, in Christ Jesus, before there can be any thought of worship. A dead man can't worship. Jesus said, "Except a man be born again, he cannot see the kingdom of God," and again "Ye must be born again" (John 3:3, 5, 7).

Once the birth from above has taken place, worship has begun. For who is truly saved who does not begin to praise the Lord at once? The very heart attitude of gratitude toward the Savior is worship. And expressed in words, by the newborn babe, it is most acceptable to the Father.

2. *Attitude of gratitude*

The maintenance of a grateful attitude toward the Lord continually demands the utmost care and cultivation. The first warmth of love and devotion to the Savior may quickly become only a memory if there isn't a constant deliverance from sin and its blighting consequences and at the same time a continual intake of Christ, the bread and water of life.

Real confession and repentance of newly committed sin in the life of a believer is absolutely necessary if true worship is to continue or to be restored. The attitude of gratitude is restored when sin is confessed and forsaken. Any believer who ceases to repent when he sins has ceased to be a worshiper. He may continue to go to church and take part in all its activities, but that inner voice of praise to God is silent, though his lips sing the hymns of praise. His worship has become a mockery.

So also is the matter of new discoveries of riches and wisdom and beauty and holiness in Christ, daily, in His inexhaustible Word. Just as surely as true worship prepares the heart for prayer, perception, and performance, so does the sincere searching of the Scriptures lead to new outbursts of praise and exaltation of our adorable Lord.

3. *Dedication*

A third vital factor in preparation for worship is that of submission of the whole man—body, soul, and spirit—to the Lord. As Joshua cast himself before the Captain of the Lord's host, he withheld nothing. To do that meant the giving up of his own will for good and forever, for the will of Another.

What takes place in such an act of surrender and

yieldedness is the establishing of a firm purpose, never to be altered, of hating sin and loving holiness. But the setting of such a life purpose is but the beginning of the battles and victories that will follow. It is one thing to make complete commitment at a given time, to the Lord. It is quite another, and most important thing, to prove that commitment, through all the days that follow. This requires the Lord's doing, for He alone is equal to it in the believer. True worship is the outcome.

4. *Fountain of joy*

True devotion springs only from a glad heart. While Jesus' body was lying in the tomb, not one of His disciples worshiped Him. They went about mourning and weeping. But the moment they saw the risen Lord, gladness filled their hearts. And that fountain of joy continued to well up as He showed Himself again and again, until the day of His ascension, as He ascended to glory. We read in Luke 24:52, 53, "And they worshiped him, and returned to Jerusalem with great joy: And were continually in the temple, praising and blessing God. Amen."

Jesus meant so much to them that they couldn't contain themselves. He was so great and wonderful to them that they had to keep praising Him and telling others about Him, so they too would overflow with His presence and joy. Where is that overflowing joy today? We must have it individually and collectively, to make us true worshipers and flaming evangelists.

How to Worship

Attempting to tell a believer how to worship the Lord he loves is a little like undertaking to prescribe for a young man how to admire, adore, and make his love known to his sweetheart. Yet the Lord tells us explicitly, in His Word, some of the things pertaining to the "how."

For instance, in Hebrews 13:15 we learn that it is done by Christ. "By him therefore let us offer the sacrifice of praise to God continually." He is not only the object of our worship but also the means. Be it love, admiration, honor, glory, or praise that we bring, He furnishes all. He put the song in our hearts and on our lips. We love Him because He first loved us.

Also, in John 4:24, He tells us, "God is a spirit: and they that worship him must worship him in spirit and in truth." To worship the Lord in spirit is not to worship Him in the flesh, or the old sinful nature. Neither is it to worship Him simply in the intellect. It is to worship Him in the highest part of us, the spirit. It is the spirit realm in which God lives, and if we, who also are spirits, seek to do Him honor, it can only be done by coming into His realm where He is. This is the work of the Holy Spirit, as we yield to Him. And to worship God in truth is to eliminate error, falsehood, imagination, and to praise Him and exalt Him in the person and power of the Holy Spirit, who is the Spirit of Truth.

Again, the way to worship God is to address Him with real intention of the whole heart. Worship does not just happen, nor is it a passive thing. Wherever it is recorded in God's Word, it is always carried on with intention in direct address to the Lord. A good example is Psalm 9:1, "I will praise thee, O LORD, with my whole heart." Notice the "I will." Many of God's children are weak and sparse in worship because they have no real intention of loving and adoring God.

Classes of Worshipers

On earth there are just two classes of worshipers, the true and the false. In heaven there is just one class, the true—both angels and people. The true worshipers on earth are God's children who are led by the Holy Spirit to hate sin and love righteousness. They seek the Lord with all their hearts. They are the true followers of Christ, who bear their cross daily and forsake all for His name's sake. They are the meek, the lowly, the humble and broken-hearted. They are the ones who rejoice in Him with joy unspeakable and full of glory.

Among God's children there are many who do very

little worshiping. Though they are born again, they do not love the Lord much, and are not growing much in the grace and knowledge of the Lord. Bible reading and prayer are more of a duty than a delight to them. There is little real joy in their hearts and the doing of God's will is not a vital issue. All such need to be helped in prayer and instruction in God's Word to see and experience the great privilege and joy of the life of Christ lived to the full, and of worshiping Him with a whole heart.

The false worshipers are all who have never come to know Christ as Savior, but who, for various reasons make along in religious things. Jesus spoke of them in Matthew 15:8, 9, "This people draweth nigh unto me with their mouth, and honoreth me with their lips; but their heart is far from me. But in vain they do worship me, teaching for doctrines the commandments of men." These think they are really worshiping the true and living God, but they are duped and deceived.

Results of Worship

Joshua never stood taller in the presence of the Lord than when he lay prostrate at His feet on Jericho's plain. There, he was wholly submissive to his God. No saint ever rises above that, though he grows and grows. Who can estimate the value of that position and place? In the New Testament it is mentioned multiplied times as being "in Christ." It covers all we can ever hope to be and do.

Briefly, three tremendous things come to mind quickly. First, Joshua, in so worshiping the Lord, gave Him His rightful place. This is giving God the glory that is due Him. That's our all-inclusive business, be it in heaven or on earth. Second, as Joshua gave God His rightful place, he put himself in his proper place, that of complete submission, so that God could use him. And in the third place, it prepared Joshua for the other three imperatives that followed in quick succession: he asked for orders (prayed), he listened for the answer and received it (perceived), and he carried out the command (performed or obeyed).

Worship, Beauty, Holiness

George Campbell Morgan (1863–1945) was the son of a British Baptist preacher and preached his first sermon when he was thirteen years old. He had no formal training for the ministry, but his tireless devotion to the study of the Bible helped him to become one of the leading Bible teachers of his day. Rejected by the Methodists, he was ordained into the Congregational ministry. He was associated with Dwight L. Moody in the Northfield Bible conferences and as an itinerant Bible teacher. He is best known as the pastor of Westminster Chapel, London (1904–17 and 1933–35). During his second term there, he had Dr. D. Martyn Lloyd-Jones as his associate. He published more than 60 books and booklets, and his sermons are found in *The Westminster Pulpit* (London, Hodder and Stoughton, 1906–16). This sermon is from Volume II.

George Campbell Morgan

10

WORSHIP, BEAUTY, HOLINESS

O worship the Lord in the beauty of holiness (Psalm 96:9).

THE WORD THAT attracts our attention in this text is the word "beauty." "O worship the Lord in the beauty of holiness." Whether in application this word is of supreme importance may be another question. The very fact of its attractiveness compels us to consider its setting. In that consideration we shall discover its suggestiveness and importance.

The particular word translated "beauty" here is used only five times in the Scriptures; once in Proverbs 14:28, where it is translated in the Authorized Version "honor," and in the Revised Version "glory"; again in 1 Chronicles 16:29; in the psalm which was sung when the ark was brought from the house of Obed-edom to its resting-place in the tent or tabernacle; again in 2 Chronicles, in the story of Jehoshaphat's arrangement of the singers who were to precede the army, who were charged in their singing to "praise the beauty of holiness"; again in Psalm 29, and in this text.

It is a somewhat rare word. Our English word "beauty" does most perfectly express the real meaning of the word, of which it is a translation. It suggests honor, or glory, or beauty, not as a decoration, but as an *intrinsic value*, an inherent quality. The Revised Version suggests in its marginal reading in each case that we should read, "Worship the Lord in holy array." But this does not interfere with the essential thought of the passage, for it cannot refer merely to material clothing, but to that outshining of inner character which is the true array of the soul in its *approach to God in worship*, that outshining of inner character which makes even sackcloth beautiful, and homespun a thing of ineffable glory. We do not forget that when our Lord was transfigured, that transfiguration was not the shining upon Him of a light from heaven, not even, as I venture to believe, the out-shining of His Deity, but rather the shining through of the essential glory and perfection of His human nature. Eye-witnesses tell us that His very raiment became white and glistening, and yet as we read the story we know that it was the appearance of the glory of a raiment due to the essential glory of His own character there manifested to them for their sakes rather than for His.

And so with our word "beauty" here, the thought is that of an inherent quality, not a decoration, not something put on as from without, but something manifest to the eye, and appealing to the emotion and the mind, as being in itself glorious and beautiful, and yet belonging essentially to the fact with which we are brought into contact. The text is a cry, calling upon men to worship, and so incidentally revealing the true nature of worship. Only once does this particular word occur apart from the same kind of setting—in the book of Proverbs. Everywhere else it is associated with worship, holiness. "O worship the Lord in the beauty of holiness."

These words lie in the midst of language in which the psalmist is appealing to men to praise God, calling them to recognize His greatness, calling them to recognize His glory, calling them to think of His power and His majesty, and urging them to answer the things their eyes see, and their hearts feel, by offering praise to Him.

Worship

In this call so poetic and full of beauty there is a revelation of the deep meaning of worship, of its abiding condition, and glory. "O worship the Lord in the beauty of holiness." The supreme thing is worship. But how is worship to be rendered? "In the beauty of holiness." Wherever you find beauty, it is the outcome of holiness. Wherever you find beauty as the outcome of holiness, that beauty in itself is incense, is worship. To attempt to worship in any other way is to fail. To live the life of holiness is to live the life of beauty, and that is to worship.

What is worship? The essential and simple meaning of the word, and therefore the fundamental thought is that of prostration, of bowing down. Worship suggests that attitude which recognizes the throne, which recognizes superiority; that attitude of the life which takes the low place of absolute reverence in the presence of that which takes hold upon the life and compels it. It is a word full of force, which constrains us, and compels us to the attitude of reverence.

The word "worship" runs through the Bible, and the thought of worship is to be found from beginning to end. The thought of worship is on the part of man, the recognition of Divine sufficiency, the recognition of his absolute dependence upon the Divine sufficiency, the confession that all he needs in his own life he finds in the life of God. And the spoken answer to that conviction of the abandonment and *surrender of the whole of man to God is worship.* I worship in the presence of God, as I recognize that in Him I find everything that my life demands, as I find that in myself I am incomplete everywhere, save as I am brought into relationship with Him. A sense of my need and His resource, a sense that all my life finds only its heights and its best, and fulfils itself in relation to Him, produces the act and the attitude of worship. *The attitude of worship is* the attitude of *a subject bent before the King.* The attitude of worship is the attitude *of a child yielding all its love to its Father.* The attitude of worship is the attitude of the *sheep that follows the leading of the Shepherd,* and is content in all that pasturage which He appoints. It is the attitude of *saying Yes to everything that God says.*

The height of worship is realized in expression in the use of two words which have never been translated, which remain upon the page of the Holy Scriptures, and in the common language of the church, as they were in the language where they originated: "Hallelujah" and "Amen." When I have learned to say those two words with all my mind, and heart, and soul, and being, I have at once found the highest place of worship, and the fullest realization of my own life. "Let all the people

praise the Lord. Let all the people say, Amen." And when
I pass on presently to the end of the Divine Library, I
hear in heaven, "a great multitude. . . saying, Hallelujah . . . . And a second time they say, Hallelujah"; and
the great responsive answer is "Amen." Amen to His
will, and Hallelujah, the offering of praise. I know it is
but a simple symbol. I know it is but the saying of an old
thing, but I address my own heart as much as any of you,
my brethren, and I say, Oh, soul of mine, hast thou
learned to say "Amen" to Him, and that upon the basis of
a deep and profound conviction of all His absolute perfection in government, and method and providence? Can
you not say, not as the boisterous shout of an un-
enlightened soul, but as the quiet expression of a heart
resting in the perfection of God, "Hallelujah" and
"Amen"? Then that is worship, that is life.

I am not going to discuss secondary worship, save to
refer to it and recognize it. The outward acts are sacred.
The songs of praise that tell of the goodness and the
grace and the sufficiency of God, the prayer that pours
out its burden because it is confident in God's resource to
meet all human need, the quiet attention to the Word of
God as we meditate upon it: these are the *outward acts of
worship*, and behind the praise and the prayer, and the
meditation upon His Word is this great consciousness
that all I need is in Him, and that in proportion as my
whole life is abandoned to Him, in that proportion my
need will be met, and so my life itself, restful in God,
powerful because of my relationship to Him, will be a
song, a psalm, an anthem; or if I may go back and borrow
the words, God's own poetry, God's own poem, the music
that glorifies Him.

So, brethren, the outward acts are the least important
parts of our worship. *If I have not been worshiping God
for the last six days, I cannot worship Him this morning.*
If there has been no song through my life to God, I am not
prepared to sing his praise, and the reason why so often

Hosannas languish on our tongues

is because "our devotion dies." This is a pause in worship,

and expresses a perpetual attitude. The worship of the sanctuary is wholly meaningless and valueless save as it is preceded by and prepared for by the worship of the life.

We may now press on to ask the meaning of the psalmist when he says, "O worship the Lord in the beauty of holiness." Let us fix our attention in the most simple way upon the word "beauty," in our common use of it.

Beauty

When Charles Kingsley lay dying, he said, among other things, "How beautiful God is!" We are almost startled by the word. We do not often think of it in that connection. We speak of His majesty. We speak of His might. We speak of His mercy. We speak of His holiness. We speak of His love. And yet, brethren, there is nothing of God which He has made more patent to men than the fact of His beauty. Every ultimate thought of God is beautiful. Every manifestation of God is full of beauty.

Do we see beauty in all things that surround us? We are so blind, and seldom see beauty, but can we not see God's handiwork, evidences of His presence and power, and God's law operating in the blossom of a perfect beauty?

My brethren, these are commonplaces to us. Yet how often do we see them? I am not here to remind you of these things. I am here to take you back to the thought of the beauty of God, blossoming in the daisy on the sod, blazing in the starry heavens, to bring you back to my text, "O worship the Lord in the beauty of holiness," to remind you of the fact that *every ultimate thought of God is beautiful*, and that ugliness and deformity are never of God. All the beauty of flowers in form and color and perfume are of God. All the beauty of the seasons as they pass: spring and summer and autumn and winter, all that is beautiful in man physically, mentally, spiritually, and all that is beautiful in the inter-relation between man and man, is of God.

To put this same truth for one moment from another standpoint, *everything which is of God is beautiful*. The marring of a flower which makes it ugly is not of God. That in a man which is repulsive is not of God. God is a God of might. God is a God of glory. God is a God of love. But He is also the God of beauty. It is well for us to think of it for a moment and remember it.

I remember staying, some years ago, while conducting some special service, with a friend in Devonshire. There came by the morning mail to him some roses wrought in silk by deft fingers here in London. And he put some of these roses wrought in silk by me, and said, "They are very beautiful." And holding them up in my folly and short-sightedness, I said, "They are perfect." He replied, "Are they, really?" And he brought his microscope, and put the rose beneath it, and the very silk itself became course as sackcloth. Then he brought from his greenhouse a spray of God's roses, and put them under the microscope, and the more closely I looked, the more perfect they were. The beauty of God as manifest in the tiniest cell of the flower as in its completion is manifest in the blossoming of the flower, as in the rhythmic order of the heavens about me. Brethren, God is very beautiful, and everything which is of God is essentially beautiful.

Holiness

Therefore, do not let us be afraid of our text when we come to the subject of holiness. "Worship the Lord in the beauty of holiness." In God's works beauty is the expression of holiness.

> The beauty is His handiwork,
>   The light glows from His face,
> The perfume is His sweetness,
>   All earth's beauty is His grace.

If God's ultimate thought is realized only along the line of His law, then the law is that which creates the beauty; and everywhere beauty is marred by the breaking of law. Holiness, then, is rectitude of character, the condition of beauty. What is "the beauty of holiness"? The realization of a Divine thought by abiding in the Divine law. That is the one and only condition of worship.

Let me illustrate again. The flowers that blossom on the sod are worshiping God. But how are they worshiping? They are worshiping by their beauty. And what is their beauty? The beauty is the result of the operation of the law of God; and in answer to the laws of their life, not by effort, not by garments other than the garments essential glory wrought out from their inner life, they worship. They worship in beauty because they worship in holiness. They worship within the realm of law. "The trees of the Lord," said one of the ancient writers, "are full," and I often regret the addition in translation which imagines that the Hebrew method of expression is so imperfect that we must add to it to complete it. Our translators have written, "The trees of the Lord are full of sap." They thought it was poetic. I think it was prosaic. I think they had been looking at a tree, and they thought there was nothing but sap. The Hebrew word is "full." Change the word "sap" to "beauty," and that would still be incomplete. There are things which are subtracted from by adding to. "The trees of the Lord are full," full of sap, full of beauty, full of health, full of poetry.

But let me introduce the word "beauty" here. "The trees of the Lord are full of beauty," and are they not? Oh, it is good to get away and stand among the trees. "The trees of the Lord are full." "The voice of the Lord breaketh the cedars." What did the psalmist mean? He says, "The God of glory thundereth . . . the Lord breaketh in pieces the cedars of Lebanon." The Word of God, the enunciation of law is upon them, and they have heard, and have answered, and in the uprising of their life, they have blossomed into fulness of form and beauty. Did you ever see an ugly tree? I have, but it was a tree some fool of a man had tried to cut into the shape of a bird. But a tree is full of beauty. What is its beauty? It is the beauty of law. You spoil the law of the tree, and you will rob it of its beauty, and you will rob God of His worship.

You may climb higher. The cloud rises in the sky, and you with your incipient infidelity grumble because the sun is shut out from your patch of earth. Presently the cloud is giving itself away, flinging itself out upon the earth; and gradually it exhausts itself, and ceases to be. Every rain shower is the worshiping of a cloud, its fulfilment of the purpose of its being. It is its answer to the movement of God in the economy of life. And as the cloud pours itself out it worships, it worships in the beauty of holiness. The tides that come and go worship, and worship in beauty, worship in majesty, the deep range of their voice roaring around us, until we are deafened, but it is all an anthem of worship. But what is their beauty? The answer to law, the fulfilling of the purpose of God.

When Does One Worship?

So we climb by these illustrations to man. When does a man worship? A man worships when he is what God meant him to be. I may sing every song in the hymnbook, and never worship. I may recite every creed that was ever prepared, and never worship. I may inflict all manner of scourging upon this body of mine, and never worship. I may kneel in long lonely vigils of the night, and never worship; and the song, and the sacrifice, and the prayer are nothing *unless I am*, in this one lonely individual life of mine, *what God Almighty meant me to be*. When I am that, my whole life worships.

How can I be that? Only as I discover His law, only as I walk in His ways; and here is the difference between the flower and man. The supreme dignity, the tremendous and overwhelming majesty of your life and mine is that of our power to choose, to elect, to decide, to will. Consequently, the worship of the soul that can choose and decide and elect and will is profounder, mightier, greater than any other worship could be. It is not in the antiphonal song of choirs, or in the chanting of music to which we listen, or even in our own singing; it is in taking hold of our individual life, and the putting of it into such relationship with God that it becomes what He means it should be.

I do not worship God by going to China as a missionary, if God wants me to stay at home and do the work of a carpenter. I do not worship God by aspiring to some mighty and heroic thing for Him, if the capacity He has given me is for doing the quiet thing, and the simple thing, and the hidden thing, and the unknown thing. It would be very foolish for the hummingbird, instead of entering the tulip, to try to beat back the air and combat with the eagle. It worships by staying where God puts it. It would be very wicked for the eagle to cultivate a mock modesty, and say that it preferred to remain among the tulips, when it ought to be soaring sunwards.

What Is Worship?

So that if I have spoken to you about the fact that God has foreordained works, that we should walk in them, I now remind you that if you worship when you find God's appointment, and when you walk in the way God has appointed, you realize your own life.

Worship consists in the finding of my own life, and the yielding of it wholly to God for the fulfilment of His purpose. That is worship!

You say, Would you tell us to find our life? Did not Jesus say we must lose it? Yes, "He that findeth his life shall lose it," but He did not finish there: "He that loseth his life for My sake shall find it," not another life, not a new life, not a new order of life, not an angel's life, for instance, but his own life. The Cross is necessary, restraint is necessary, sacrifice is necessary, self-denial is necessary; but these things are all preliminary, and when Paul describes the Christian life at its fullest, he does not say, I am crucified. That is the wicket gate, that is the pathway that leads out, that is the beginning. "I have been crucified with Christ: yet I live; and yet no longer I, but Christ liveth in me: and that life which I now live in the flesh I live in faith, the faith which is in the Son of God."

Or again, he says, speaking of Christ Himself, "It is Christ that died," but that is not the last thing, nor the final thing, "yea rather, that was raised from the dead."

And so if the Cross be absolutely necessary, and it is, your cross, my cross, my individual dying to the ambitions of selfish desire, all that is necessary; but beyond it, life. What life? My life. The new birth is but the passing into the possibility of the first birth. The new creation is but the finding of the meaning of, and the fulfilment of the purposes of the first creation. "O worship the Lord in the beauty of holiness." Discover His law, answer His law, walk in the way of His appointing. Let Him who made you lead out all the facts of your life to the fulfilment of His purpose, and then your whole life is worship.

Then, brethren, you will see that worship does not begin when you go to church. This is a very valuable part of worship, but it is secondary worship, symbolic worship. This is the day in which we cease the worship that perfectly glorifies Him in order that in song and praise and prayer we may remind ourselves of the perpetual and unending truth that life lived within His will, and according to His law, the life of holiness is the beauty that glorifies God. This service is but a pause in which in word and attitude we give expression to life's inner song. And if there be no such inner song, there is no worship here. Worship is the perpetual poetry of Divine power and Divine love expressed in human life.

Angels worship not merely when veiling their faces they sing of His holiness, but when ceasing their singing at His bidding, they fly to catch the live coal from the altar, and touch the lips of a penitent soul who sighs. It is true "they also serve who only stand and wait." But it is equally true that they also worship who serve, and serve perpetually. And it is in the service of a life, not specific acts done as apart from the life, not because I teach in Sunday school, or preach here, that I worship. I may preach here today, and never worship. But because my life is found in His law, is answering His call, responsive to His provision and arrangement, so almost, without knowing it, my life has become a song, a praise, an anthem. So I worship! I join the angels, and all nature, in worship when I become what God intends I should be.

And in that blossoming of His ideal we sing the song of His greatness and His love.

> Our midnight is Thy smile withdrawn;
> Our noontide is Thy gracious dawn;
> Our rainbow arch, Thy mercy's sign;
> All save the clouds of sin are Thine.
>
> Grant us Thy Truth to make us free,
> And kindling hearts that burn for Thee,
> Till all Thy living altars claim
> One holy Light, one heavenly flame.

And so I pray that when the service is over, and Sunday has passed, we may know that in the shop, in the office, in the home and market place, in all the toil of the commonplaces, we can worship the Lord in the beauty of holiness. Where there is holiness there is beauty. Where there is beauty there is worship. However ornate the worship may be in external things, if it lacks the beauty of holiness, it never reaches the inner sanctuary, and never glorifies God.

Adoration

Henry Parry Liddon (1829–1890) belonged to the High Church school of the Anglican Church. Ordained in 1853, he served in two brief pastorates and as vice-principal of a school. He moved to Oxford and there preached to large crowds at St. Mary's and Christ Church. He is perhaps best known for his Bampton Lectures, *The Divinity of Our Lord and Savior Jesus Christ*. From 1870 to his death, he was canon of St. Paul's Cathedral, London, which he sought to make into an Anglican preaching center to rival Charles Spurgeon's Metropolitan Tabernacle. This sermon comes from Vol. 1 of "The Contemporary Pulpit Library," *Sermons by H. P. Liddon*, published in London, in 1897, by Swan Sonneschein & Co.

Henry Parry Liddon

11

ADORATION

O come, let us worship and bow down, and kneel before the Lord our Maker" (Psalm 95:6).

THESE WORDS WILL BE very familiar to all church-goers, because they occur in the psalm which always forms part of the morning's service. This psalm is still used in the Friday evening service of the Jewish synagogue as an invitation to the duties of the Sabbath; and the western church of Christ from very early times has sung it, as the Church of England sings it to this day, as an introduction to daily worship. No other psalm is so frequently used in the English Prayerbook, and the reason for the prominence thus assigned to it is probably twofold.

First, although in its original form it may have been written by David, it bears traces of having been expanded and adapted by some other inspired writer for use as an introit or introduction at some one of the temple services; and, secondly, the New Testament marks out this psalm for special distinction, since in the Epistle to the Hebrews more of its verses are quoted and commented upon than is the case with any other psalm. Such a psalm necessarily suggests a great many subjects of interest; but the point to which the text directs our attention is the import and value of its invitation to worship: "O come, let us worship and fall down, and kneel before the Lord our Maker."

Now if you look at the psalm, you will see that it contains two strophes or stanzas: the first consisting of five verses and the second of six. Each of these stanzas opens with an invitation. The first is an invitation to praise offered loudly with the voice. Literally rendered it runs thus: "O come, let us shout joyfully to the Lord: let us make a joyful noise to the Rock of our salvation; let us go forth to meet Him with thanksgiving; let us make a joyful noise to Him with hymns." And the second stanza

begins with an invitation to something altogether different: to worship, or as we had better render it, to adoration. This invitation is conveyed by words which, rendered literally, would run thus: "O come, let us prostrate
ourselves, let us bow down, let us kneel before the Lord
our Maker." The word which is rendered "worship"
means prostration, literally nothing less than
prostration.

The two words which follow mean something less emphatic. The first, the bending of the body while the
worshiper still stands, the second, kneeling. Nothing
changes in the East so far as habit is concerned, and you
cannot today enter a mosque without seeing each of
these three words literally acted upon. Sometimes the
worshiper bends his head and shoulders, then he kneels,
then he prostrates himself entirely, touching the ground
with his forehead. This, so far as the outward posture
goes, is undoubtedly what the Psalmist meant to invite
the congregation of Israel to do, as being the outward
expression of adoration. But adoration is an inward act
of the soul which corresponds with those postures of the
body which have just been described. It is the soul recog-
nizing its nothingness before the magnificence of God,
its sin before His purity, its ignorance before His omnis-
cience, its feebleness before His power. It is the creature
lying in the dust and understanding, as by a flash of
light from heaven, what it is to have been created, what
it is to have a Creator and to be alive in His presence. It is
sinful man emptying himself of self-assertion before the
Being who made him, knowing himself, or almost knowing himself as he is known, crying: "Out of the deep have
I called unto Thee, O Lord, out of the deep of my sinfulness to Thy perfect holiness, out of the deep of my folly to
Thy infinite wisdom, out of the deep of my weakness to
Thy boundless power,—out of the deep have I called to
Thee, the All-mighty, the All-wise, the All-good: Lord,
hear my voice."

Adoration in Religion

Every false religion has some sustaining truth in it,

and the truth which is especially recognized by Mohammedanism is that which is implied in adoration. The
name by which this religion is known throughout the
East is a most vivid and beautiful word, which touches
the universal conscience of mankind. "Islam" means subjection – the subjection of the creature to the Creator, the
subjection of man to God. It is not now our business to
inquire how far in practice Mohammedanism realizes
the moral expectations which are raised by its distinc-
tive name. The name itself is based on a truth which
certainly does not concern us Christians less than other
people. The name "Islam" shines with a moral light to
which we, the servants of Christ, cannot close our eyes.
Who can doubt that side by side with the ruthless scimitar, which proved so terribly effective a missionary in
the hands of the early followers of the Arabian prophet,
this pregnant and inspiring word "Islam" did its work in
many a noble soul, attracting it powerfully to a religion
of which the central and fundamental feature seemed to
be nothing else or less than the insistence on the true
attitude of man to Almighty God? Nor, so far as the
attitude of worship goes, does the practice of religious
Moslems belie their profession. As has been said, Mohammedanism contains features to which Christianity
is vitally opposed.

We do not forget that the moral system of the Koran on
the better side is only a reflex of the natural nobility of
the Arab character; on its worst side, it is a deliberate
compromise with, if it be not rather a surrender to, the
strongest and most destructive passions of our fallen
nature. We do not forget that in Mohammedanism our
Lord Jesus Christ is considered a prophet, ranking
below Mohammed, but with Adam, Abraham and Moses,
nevertheless, His divinity, His co-equality with the Father, is insolently rejected in those very verses of Koran
which are inscribed in large letters around the Mosque
of the Dome of the Rock at Jerusalem, as if to bid defiance to the central truth of the Christian creed on the
very spot which, next to the sites of the nativity, the
crucifixion, and the resurrection, is holiest in Christian

eyes. We do not forget this. Yet let us do justice to the manner in which the religious Moslem rejoices to acknowledge the claims of God, so far as he understands them. Five times a day from the minaret does the Muezzin proclaim the call to prayer. Not seldom during the still hours of the night is this call heard sounding above the towers of an Eastern city, and inviting the faithful who are still awake to rise and pray. And in early morning, and as the sun sets, and in the busiest hours of the day, all else gives way to the duty, the supreme duty, of publicly acknowledging the sovereignty of God. In the fields, in the bazaar, in the barrack room, or on the deck of the crowded steamboat, not less than in the mosque or in the home, the devout Moslem will unwrap his carpet, consecrating thereby, as he conceives, one spot on earth to the most solemn of its duties, and utterly regardless of the wonder or of the sneers of bystanders, will he prostrate himself, with the evident sincerity of utter self-abasement, before the inaccessible majesty of the one Omnipotent and Eternal Being.

No Christian can watch this spectacle unmoved, or without a certain feeling of compunction or self-reproach. If that narrow and arid conception of God which is all that really meets the student in the pages of the Koran can draw forth from the heart of these poor Moslems this passionate devotion, what ought to be the case with us, who know God in His blessed Son, who survey in the light of His one certain and outward revelation of Himself the whole range of His glorious attributes; who, if we would only understand our privileges, are flooded with light, since we are at His feet in Whom are hid all the treasures of wisdom and knowledge? What should our practice be? What is it? May it not be that, in the eyes of that unerring Justice which eighteen centuries ago summoned the men of Nineveh and the Queen of the South to rise in judgment against the generation which listened to Him, but listened to Him without profit, many of us Christians, too, may stand condemned by our failure to render the tribute of adoration to Him who has redeemed and sanctified, as well as created us, by the practice of those very Mohammedans whom our missionaries would fain convert to Christianity by faith in Jesus Christ as Son of God?

Adoration and Admiration

In the strictness of the word, adoration is an expression by an outward, but much more by an inward act, of man's sincere conviction that his first duty to Almighty God is submission. And thus it is distinct from many other acts of the soul which are sometimes apt to be mistaken for it. Contrast it, for example, with admiration. Many people in our day seem to think that a sincere and very warm admiration of God will do as well, or almost as well, as adoring Him. They see beautiful scenery, or they trace, or think they trace, a particular motive at work in the course of human events. Or they read a book of astronomy, and for the moment they are interested in the distances and the magnitude of the fixed stars; or they are students of the laws of human thought, and they are too sensible to suppose that those laws can be accounted for by supposing them to have been somehow evolved from some original, self-existent paste.

Brethren, these persons are on the right road to go much further than admiration. They are, if they only knew it, on the road to adoration, but they do somehow content themselves with admiring God. They say many fine and true things about the Author of the material and intellectual universe which so greatly interests them, but then they say just as much about it as about its Author. If all that is to be given to God is the enthusiasm which we bestow on a beautiful flower, or on a grand mountain, or on a splendid poem, it is clear that, however warmly we may admire, we are a long way from adoration. As admirers, mark this, we are taking it for granted that we are so far on a level with the object admired as to be able to do Him justice; as admirers we presuppose and exercise, although favorably, our rights as critics. In adoration, we abandon utterly all such pretensions as profane, as grotesque; we have no thought but that of God's solitary and awful greatness, and of our own utter insignificance before Him.

Adoration, Thanksgiving, Praise and Prayer

Adoration, then, is not, in any serious sense, devotion. But compare adoration with the other acts of the soul which do undoubtedly belong to devotion. When we assemble and meet together in church, it is, as we are daily reminded, to "render thanks for the great benefits that we have received at God's hands, to set forth His most worthy praise, to hear His most holy word, and to ask those things which are requisite and necessary as well for the body as the soul." Of these four objects of assembling together in church, that of hearing God's Word, whether read or preached, is not now in question.

But what is the relation of the other three, thanksgiving, praise, and prayer for blessings, to adoration? They all three differ from adoration in this, that in each of them the soul is less prostrate, more able to bear the thought of self, than in pure and simple adoration? Certainly, in praise we seem to forget self more easily than in thanksgiving or prayer, since thanksgiving carries the mind back to something which we have received, and by which presumably we have profited, and prayer, in the narrower sense of the word, asks for new blessings, whether for the body or soul. Pure adoration had no heart for self; it lies there silent at the foot of the throne, conscious only of two things, the insignificance of self and the greatness of God. And yet adoration must be the basis, so to put it, of true thanksgiving and praise and prayer; it is the fitting acknowledgment of our real relations with God, which should precede them. It sometimes does, indeed, imply so paralyzing a sense of this our nothingness before God that left to itself it would make praise, thanksgiving, and prayer impossible. But here, as we lie in the dust, the one Mediator between God and man bids us take heart as He utters that most consoling sentence: "No man cometh unto the Father but by Me" (John 14:6). He bids us, as it were, take His hand, and thus, with Him and by Him, not merely adore God, but praise Him, thank Him, pray to Him. Prayer, we know, is effectual when it is offered in His prevailing name. "Whatsoever ye shall ask the Father in My name, He will give it to you" (John 15:16).

Praise is accepted when it is associated with Him by whom and with whom, in the unity of the Holy Spirit, all glory and honor is rendered unto God, the Father Almighty. Thanksgiving is welcomed when it is offered in union with Him who is the one Thankoffering of Christendom, no less than its one propitiatory Sacrifice, especially when it is offered in that most solemn of all services that are possible on earth, in which we venture most daringly into the very presence-chamber of the Heavens, because leaning on a strength and covered with a righteousness which most assuredly is not our own. But until our Lord and Savior thus takes us by the hand, adoration, the most distant and the most lowly, of the Infinite and Almighty God is all that is, seriously speaking, open to us. And when He has thus taken us by the hand, and has taught us to thank, praise and pray to God in virtue of the strength which flows from union with Himself, adoration still remains; it remains as the expression of our original and permanent relation as creatures at the footstool of the Creator. "O come, let us prostrate ourselves, let us bend low, let us fall before the Lord our Maker," is addressed to all human souls for all time.

In our common language, worship, no doubt, is not thus accurately distinguished from praise, thanksgiving and prayer. It is understood to include them. It is understood to mean not adoration proper, but the whole series of acts which make up the devotional duty of the soul to Almighty God. The psalmist's words do not mean as much as this, but we are not doing him a wrong if we consider them in a light of this popular paraphrase, which may, indeed, be largely justified by a reference to the opening verses of the psalm. Now in our day there is a disposition abroad, even, among those who do not professedly reject revealed religion, to speak disparagingly of worship, even when taken in this larger sense. Worship is treated as the indulgence of a sentiment rather than as the discharge of a sacred and imperative duty, and it is implied that too much is made of it in the system and practice of the Christian church. The church, according to one of these theorists, ought to be a great society for the social and political improvement of mankind, whereas it is little better than what he contemptuously calls an organization for worship. Worship, he contends – if not in terms, yet by implication – ought to be only the by-play of a really vigorous and living church, whereas worship seems to be the main concern of the actual Christian church, as it has been of the church of bygone days.

No Christian would wish to undervalue the social duties of the Christian church; its duties, I mean, in the way of promoting improvement in the outward and material life of the people. But they are not its most important duties, as they would be undoubtedly if men had no souls, and if there were no certainty about the eternal future, and if, as is very unlikely under these circumstances, anything that could be called a church were in existence. They are not its most important duties, but, as a matter of fact, the idea that we have such duties at all is, in the main, a creation of the Christian church. In particular, philanthropy, as we witness it today, is a product of the church's sense of social duty. It is the modern successor of those miracles of healing which won the hearts of the Galilean peasantry eighteen hundred years ago. But just as our Lord's works of mercy on the bodies of men were not either the main object or the most distinguishing feature of His ministry, so the social benefits conferred by the church of Christ are not the main objects or ornaments of her mission to mankind. Her first business is to get the souls of men saved by bringing them to their Lord and Savior, and, so far as possible, to promote their sanctification through the ministries of His Spirit. Then, in subordination to this end, and as an auxiliary to it, to do what she may for their temporal well-being. But if men's souls are to be saved, *worship*, both public and private, *is indispensable.* It is much more necessary to the church's life than any sort or kind of social improvement that can be named, and to disparage worship is to strike a blow at the very heart of the church. It is, literally, to cut up and kill the roots of the tree of Christian activity.

Benefits of Worship

Let us, then, briefly remind ourselves of some leading benefits of worship, which explain the importance which is assigned to it by the church of Christ. First of all, *it places us,* both as individuals and as a body of men, *in our true place before God, our Creator.* Unless, or until, we believe that one Being exists to whom we stand in a relation utterly different from that in which we stand to any other—namely, that of owing our very existence to Him—worship is impossible. "Be ye sure that the Lord, He is God: it is He that hath made us and not we ourselves,"—this is the certainty which lies at the basis of worship. We cannot worship some shadow of the world of thought; we cannot bow down before a theory or hypothesis as to the origin of things. Unless we "believe in one God, the Father Almighty, Maker of heaven and earth, and of all things visible and invisible," worship cannot be. It only begins when faith acknowledges the Almighty Creator. It dies away as faith in Him decays; it dies away as He gives place in thought to some purely human imagination respecting how the universe came to be what it actually is.

But even where there is no difficulty in believing in God the Creator, and no disposition to question His existence or His power, we sometimes observe that this great belief has no practical effect whatever upon life and thought. We constantly see men—it may be that we ourselves, some of us, are among the number—who never seriously consider what it is to have a Creator. Active, enterprising men, full of energy, conscious of power, still in tolerably good health, accustomed to have their own way more or less among their fellows, do not readily admit to themselves the bearing of the hard fact that one Being exists by whose will it is that they themselves exist at all, and that their existence is continued to them from moment to moment. If you say to one of them: "Do you believe in a Creator?" he would say, "Of course, I do;" but practically the world of sense is so engrossing, so importunate, that it crushes this faith back into a remote corner of the soul. Many such men practically live as though it were not true that it is God Who has made us and not we ourselves.

Now the corrective to this, which is a practical failure, after all, rather than an intellectual mistake, is worship. Worship places us face to face with the greatness of the Creator. It puts us, as we contemplate Him, out of heart with ourselves, with our own rights, with our own pretensions. We have, it may be, to confess to Him, "other gods besides Thee have had dominion over us," but the very first effort of worship implies that God is resuming, has resumed, His true place in our thoughts, that He is no longer jostled out of our mental life by a hundred, puny worthless rivals belonging to the world of sense. We cannot be practically forgetting what it is to have a Creator, when we sincerely obey the invitation to "come and worship and fall down and kneel before Him."

Worship, too, obliges us to think what we are ourselves. It is one thing to hold the immortality of man as an abstract tenet, it is another to be looking forward with a steady, practical aim to a life to come. When we worship we pass inside the veil of sense, we cross the threshold of the unseen world, we enter upon an exercise which is itself a preparation for the life which lies before us after this is over. We bow down before the majesty of God, but we also understand something of the meaning of our own existence. Who are we, that we should thus venture into His presence-chamber, if we are indeed only the creatures of a day, only beings of flesh and blood, whose life is bounded by an earthly horizon? Surely, this action of worship, in which the brutes do not participate, implies the truth which lies so deep in the minds of men, the truth of an immortal destiny. Worship, is the great preparation for another life; a waste of time, no doubt, if the soul dies with the perishing body, if decay be succeeded by no resurrection, but a use of time than which none can be more sensible, more legitimate, if there is a most certain hereafter, and if while "the things that are seen are temporal, the things that are not seen are eternal."

And thus, lastly, *worship is a stimulus to action, when,* and, of course, only when, *it is sincere.* If it is true that "to work is to pray," it is also true that to pray is to work. Prayer is, in fact, work, since it makes a large demand upon the energies of the soul, and it creates and trains in us capacity for other kinds of work than itself. It not only illuminates the understanding and enkindles the affection; it braces, it invigorates the will. In this it has a precisely opposite effect to that which may be sometimes traced to an exaggerated fondness for books of imagination. Certain kinds of novels, for instance, do enfeeble the will, by rousing us to take a keen interest in that which we know all the while has no existence whatever in fact, and thus we spend our little stock of moral force on recognized unreality, or as the apostle would put it, to "beat the air." In worship we are in contact with the most real of all beings—with Him on whose will all else strictly depends, and in comparison with whom the most solid matter in His universe is but an unsubstantial shadow. This contact with the highest reality cannot but brace us, and accordingly we find in all ages that the noblest resolves to act or to suffer have again and again been formed, as though in obedience to what seems a sudden overpowering flash of light, during worship. So it was with Isaiah when, in the year that King Uzziah died, he saw the vision in the temple: "I heard the voice of the Lord, saying, Whom shall I send, and who will go for us? Then said I, Here am I, send me" (Isa. 6:8). So it has been with more than one enterprise in our own day—the original resolution to make the venture has dated from a half-hour of sincere worship, in which the energies of a single character have been lifted above their average level, so that it became natural and easy to remove the mountain obstacles that had barred the way to action.

And this will explain the connection of this exhortation to worship in this ninety-fifth Psalm with the sudden warning which follows. It may have struck us as unintelligibly abrupt when the psalmist, after exclaiming: "O come, let us worship and fall down, and kneel before the Lord our Maker; for He is the Lord our God, and we are the people of His pasture and the sheep of His hand," suddenly proceeds: "Today, if ye will hear His voice, harden not your hearts" (Ps. 95:6–8). We fail, at first, to see the connection between that earnest exhortation to worship and this sudden, this startling warning against disobedience. But it lies precisely in the fact that we are considering, the fact that worship is apt to be a time and season of some special appeal from on high to the sense of duty, an appeal which, as free agents, we may disregard, or we may obey, at choice. "Today, if ye will hear His voice, harden not your heart, as in the provocation, and as in the day of temptation in the wilderness." The apostle, we remember, reminds Christians that they too may be guilty of the sins of unbelief and disobedience such as those of Israel when so immediately in God's presence at Massah and Meribah; that before them, too, there is the Promised Land, into which they may, after all, never enter. But this illustrates the moral invigoration which does, if we are not hardening our hearts, accompany sincere worship, just as restored health of body naturally results from a visit to the seaside or to a mountain district, unless bad habits or wilful neglect make recovery impossible.

Such considerations – apart from what is due to God as God, apart from the answers that are vouchsafed to prayer – may help to remove the mistaken idea that the importance assigned to worship in the public system of the church of Christ is a sort of corruption of the true purpose of Christianity. In truth, it would be better for all of us if we could more frequently and more earnestly comply with the Psalmist's invitation. Life is given us that we may learn our true relations with its Author, and may prepare to live with Him forever. In another world we shall probably look back upon the way in which we have spent much of our time here with deep, though unavailing, regret; but we may be sure that no such regret will ever be felt on account of any time that has been devoted to the worship of our Creator, Redeemer, and Sanctifier.

Praise

Andrew A. Bonar (1810–1892) is perhaps best
known as the friend and biographer of Robert Murray
McCheyne, and the brother of Horatius Bonar,
Scotland's poet-preacher and author of over six hundred
hymns. A minister of the Free Church of Scotland,
Andrew Bonar emphasized the devotional life and was
recognized for the depth of his prayer ministry. A
zealous premillennialist, he had a keen interest in the
plight of the Jews and, in 1839, accompanied McCheyne
on an official ministerial commission to the Holy Land.
The sermon "Praise" is from his book *Sheaves After
Harvest*, compiled by his daughters and published
posthumously in London by Pickering and Inglis.

Andrew A. Bonar

12

PRAISE

Praise ye the Lord: for it is good to sing praises unto our God; for it is pleasant; and praise is comely (Psalm 147:1).

NOTICE THAT BEAUTIFUL SCENE of worship in Revelation 5:6–13, where the four living beings and the four and twenty elders lifted up their golden vials full of odors, which are the prayers of saints. They did so in the sight of Christ—the Lamb, and yet the Lion of the tribe of Judah—appearing with the seven-sealed book in His possession, His claim to the possession of our earth as its only rightful king. On that occasion they held up their vials of prayer, as if saying, Now, Lord, in this Thy day, remember what has been unanswered hitherto. But on that same occasion we are told that they held in the other hand "every one of them a harp," all the while that they showed him the vials full of odors. And what do we learn from this, taking these four living beings and the four and twenty elders, as showing us the Church of God (the saints, I believe, of the Old Testament and the New Testament in one) every one of them holding a harp, just as really as every one of them had a vial full of odors? Is it not the illustration of the text, "Let us offer to Him the sacrifice of praise continually," just as elsewhere it is written, "Pray without ceasing"? Let us offer "praise continually, even the fruit of our lips giving thanks to His name" (Heb. 13:15). The praise we are to offer is lips—ever uttering forth thanks to His name.

In the North of Scotland, in the county of Banffshire, some years ago, there was a remarkable wave of blessing which passed from village to village on the seacoast, as if the Lord had a peculiar love for fishermen, remembering the fisherman of Galilee. At this period, three friends were visiting some of these villages. After they had gone through several of them, they came in the evening to one with a population of about five hundred souls. They said to some of the people, "Might we not have a prayer meeting?" The answer they got took them quite by surprise. "Oh, sir, it is all praise here just now. It is all praise." So the friends say, "How? What has happened to you, especially?" The answer was, "Among the adult population there are only four persons that do not profess to have been brought to Christ, and so it is all praise with us here."

Praise Begins

You see what gives origin to praise; you see where praise, and when praise, really begins. When God takes the sinner out of the miry clay, and when he sets his feet upon the rock, it is then he begins to sing the new song. You may have joined in many a tune, you may have been delighted with many a hymn, but you have never offered praise all your life long to this moment, unless your feet have been taken out of the miry clay and set upon the rock. The new song begins on THE ROCK. And it is a new song. There is not a believer here but will tell you how differently he felt from the moment he saw his Savior, and how completely different was his song of praise onward from that hour. Have you, then, got into the right position for praise? Are your feet upon the rock? "O, Lord," says Isaiah, "I will praise Thee; though Thou wast angry with me, Thine anger is turned away" (Isa. 12:1). See again where praise begins, and what kindles its flame.

There is a very beautiful incident—I do not know if it is often noticed—in the Second Book of Chronicles, chapter 29, in the history of King Hezekiah. He was led to appoint certain arrangements in regard to what we should call the psalmody of the Temple, and one of them is thus stated, "When the burnt offering began, the song of the Lord began also" (v. 27). He appointed that every morning when the sacrifice should be offered, they should sing and blow the trumpets, that all Jerusalem might know that the atoning sacrifice was now presented on Israel's altar. When the offering began, then the song of the Lord began. Again, you see there that true praise begins when the sinner's eye rests upon the sacrifice, when the guilty conscience has felt the power of the atoning blood, and when the sinner's vacant heart has been filled with the Person of the great Sacrifice, the Great Atoner Himself.

Praise Is to Be Continued

We suggested that praise is to be offered continually. It is so written (Heb. 13:15) "continually." We should count it our privilege to be in this continual frame of praise. Does not Psalm 119:164 put it in this way? "Seven times a day do I praise Thee." David says in another psalm, "I pray to Thee at evening, morning, and at noon;" but here it is, "I will praise Thee seven times a day," as if he would even go beyond the other limit in the matter of praise. At all events, we are to be praising continually.

There is no need to fear that we shall want matter, and yet is it not a fact that we do not keep up the freshness of our new song as years go on? And why is this? Is it not because we are not getting a fresh view of the Lamb of God? You observe in a very memorable chapter, the fifth of Revelation, that when they got that new sight of the Lamb, the Lamb with the Book in His possession, holding it up in their view, it is said they sang a new song. "Thou art worthy, for Thou wast slain." I appeal to believers if this is not the case, that every time they get another view of Christ, of His person, of His offering, of His office, of His words, and of His ways, then it is they feel they can sing afresh with their whole soul to Him. And is there no matter in His varied dealings with you personally, as well as endless variety in His varied manifestations of His name?

Praise Is Not Monotonous

But there is a passage, which, perhaps, might seem to a superficial reader to represent the worship in heaven, the praise in heaven, as if it were somewhat monotonous; for one seraph cried to another, says Isaiah in his sixth chapter, "Holy, holy, holy, Lord God of Hosts," and the living beings in the fourth chapter of the Revelation, full of eyes before and behind (intimating a power to look far into the mystery of godliness), are said to rest not day nor night, singing what? Singing this song, "Holy, holy, holy, Lord God Almighty." Now the question arises, Do they always sing that song? Is there no variety? Here, friends, it is good to get some right idea of what that really teaches. You are to pray without ceasing, and to praise without ceasing, "continually;" that is, your heart is to be in that state. You are filled with the groanings that cannot be uttered, and your heart is at the same time in that state, that if the chord only be touched, it is ready to give forth some utterance of adoration.

Now in the passage I have referred to, we are taught that while there may, and will be, a ceaseless variety of subjects for praise to God, yet there pervades the adoration an undertone, and the undertone is, "Holy, holy, holy." There is no levity in the praise of Heaven, there is no lightness in the hymns; they never forget all their songs to sing to the Holy, Holy, Holy One. Oh, there is glorious solemnity in heaven, glorious solemnity amid the rapturous joy of these adoring multitudes! A model surely for us. There should be no levity in our songs. Let our souls be like the seraphs, and like these living beings, who always keep before them the *holy one,* while they worship the Lamb.

Now, there are many things that might be said about praise; but you remember the Psalms have given us three statements that may guide us. The Book of Psalms says praise is *pleasant*; it says again, "it is *good* to sing praise"; and again it says "praise is *comely* for the upright."

Praise Is "Pleasant"

You know it is pleasant to yourselves; but "praise is pleasant," means more than that. It means it is pleasant to God; it is something that God is pleased with. I should like to show you how truly God takes pleasure in the praises of His saints. Have you not noticed that though Solomon offered up that remarkable prayer in the Temple in 2 Chronicles 6, recorded by the Holy Spirit, yet the blessing did not come down then. It was a little later, when the multitude of singers were as one in giving forth their praise, and saying, "The Lord is good; His mercy endureth for ever" (2 Chron. 7:3). The cloud of glory came down and filled the Temple as they uttered the burst of praise. And in the history of King Jehoshaphat (2 Chron. 20) going forth to battle against Ammon, Moab, and Seir, Jehoshaphat's remarkable prayer is recorded at full length. Still, it was not then that the victory, or the assurance of victory came; but as he marched out of Jerusalem down the valley of Tekoa, to where he expected to meet the enemy, they made the valley resound with songs. It is said he consulted with the people, and instead of going forth with common martial music, they agreed they would march down the valley with the Lord's song on their lips: and the burden of it is, "for He is good, for His mercy endureth for ever." Now, it is added, that when the song began "the Lord set an ambushment against Moab, and Ammon, and Seir" (2 Chron. 20:22), and Israel did not need to fight; they just came up and gathered the spoils.

Do you see the honor God put upon true praise rendered to Himself? Prayer must be followed by praise. Prayer by itself (the Lord seems to say) is very well, but He wants praise: He must have the harp as well as the golden vial full of odor. *We* must now have both, as well as those that stand before the Lamb.

And in the prison of Philippi, what do we find? There were Paul and Silas praying. Yes, but they "sang praises," and the emphasis is put upon the praises, for it is said the prisoners heard them, or more correctly, at least, more emphatically, it is, "and the prisoners were listening." You can, as it were, picture them awakening, and expressing wonder to each other, and each putting his ear to the door of his cell. The prisoners were listening! Songs in a prison? Such songs—songs of Zion—had never been heard there before. And it was then that the earthquake shook the prison; and the Lord came down and converted the jailer, a man memorable in the Church of God, and who will be memorable till the Lord comes. Praise is "pleasant" to the Lord, as well as pleasing to us.

Praise Is "Good"

Praise is "good"; it is sanctifying. There is something in it tending to build up the soul in sanctification. How could it be otherwise? Praise is the element of heaven. If so, in this praise there must be much of heaven. What are some of the elements of heaven? Surely one is joy — holy joy, joy in the Lord. Now, nothing sanctifies more than this joy. Mere sorrow never sanctifies; sorrow, indeed, turns us away from earthly good, but in itself the sorrow of the world worketh death. What sanctifies?

These light afflictions, which are but for a moment, work out for us an exceeding weight of glory, while we look not at the things that are seen, but at the things that are not seen (2 Cor. 4:17, 18). It is joy to which we are led by sorrow that sanctifies — joy in the Lord, joy that is the element of heaven.

And we can at once see there is something unselfish in praise. You can suppose prayer to have a great deal of selfishness in it, and the Lord is quite aware of that; but He does not object to a kind of selfishness in our prayers, that is, that kind of seeking that we ourselves may be receivers of His blessing. But praise is more unselfish, more heaven-like, more, therefore, like Jesus; it is a giving forth of what we have received. And further — I think you will all agree in this, only sing praise truly, and there will be little discontent. I do not know a better remedy for discontent than praise, true praise. Where are your murmurs when you are singing praise? Oh, if those that fret and are discontented at little things or at great things, if they would only substitute for all that, praise, they would soon know it is good to give thanks! Oh, praise is sanctifying! Praise chases away hard thoughts of God which men call "infirmities," and which saints often call "infirmities," but which are really downright corruption, and dishonoring to God, as much as were the murmurs in the camp of Israel.

Praise Is "Comely"

And then praise is "comely." I will not dwell upon this. But you will at once own that praise is very becoming. Only withhold it and you will see what a position you put yourself into. Ask, Is it right to withhold praise? Would it be grateful? Would you feel as if you were putting yourself in a right position? A good man once said, with something of sarcasm, "I think some Christian people are going to make heaven a place of gratitude, and mean to keep all their gratitude until they get there, they show so little here." Praise is comely. To withhold it is most unseemly. Most unseemly in any circumstances; for it matters not what your position is as a saint of God, or your position in the world, or what your afflictions may be, or what your circumstances, praise is still fitting. Every Christian is expected, in all circumstances, to be able to praise continually. All believers, remember. But yet, it is not the case that all saints always do it. One of our old Scots writers, John Livingstone, said in his day, "A line of praise is worth a page of prayer," because he found it such a rare thing. Do you think he exaggerated? He wanted to stir up believers to praise more. And you notice in the Book of Psalms, as it gets near its close, prayer is "almost" forgotten. The four last Psalms are just a burst of praise. The stream is spread: it is not shallower, it is deeper, but it is just joining the ocean, and it is all praise, praise to God.

I would say further, Are you afflicted? You could not do wrong in singing praise. We heard the story of a Welsh girl whose father had died, and the mother came out of the room weeping. The child said, "Mother, what is the matter?" "Oh, what shall I do, my child? Oh, what shall I do?" "Mother, what is the matter?" "Your father is dead, child, and what shall I do?" The child looked up

into the mother's face, and said, "Mother, praise the
Lord, praise the Lord." The mother was reproved; she
went away, and she tried to praise; and as she began
to praise the Lord for what was left to her, she soon
found that the burden of her heart was lifted. The Lord
was left; the Lord with all His grace was still her possession. She was in the position of Habakkuk, who sings,
"Though the fig tree shall not blossom, neither shall
fruit be in the vines; the labor of the olive shall fail, and
the fields shall yield no meat; the flock shall be cut off
from the fold, and there shall be no herd in the stalls, yet
I will rejoice in the Lord, I will joy in the God of my
salvation" (Heb. 3:17, 18). And then he inscribed his
song, "To the chief singer upon my stringed instru-
ments." Was not that a pattern for us? Afflicted one,
praise the Lord, and tell your afflicted friends to try
praising the Lord.

I would say again, have you some special duty on
hand? Then try praise as a preface. You know what they
do when armies march. What did the Germans do lately?
What did the French do? Had they not got a military
song? Did not the Germans sing the "Watch on the
Rhine"? And did not the French sing the "Marseillaise"?
What should Christian armies do? What did our Captain
do before He went to the Mount of Olives, and as He went
to the Garden of Gethsemane, the sorest of His conflicts?
He sang a hymn—the Master sang a hymn with His
disciples. We are almost sure what it was; it was the
118th Psalm, for that was the Psalm with which the
Passover service concluded; in that Psalm you find this
burst of praise (think of the Master singing it): "The
right hand of the Lord doeth valiantly. The right hand of
the Lord is exalted: the right hand of the Lord doeth
valiantly. I shall not die but live" (Ps. 118:16, 17). Oh, try
that when going out to battle, to duties! In facing difficulties, try praise.

Again, are there anxious souls present today? I wish
you to notice, anxious soul, that this subject speaks to
you. Try praise! But I want to guard myself against
being misunderstood, for I thoroughly agree with what

has been sometimes so well stated, that in our day, there are many persons prayed into peace, and there are a great number sung into peace, and the peace is worth nothing. It is excitement; it is not peace founded on the Word, it is peace founded on the feelings. That kind of peace, whether you got it in one way or the other, if it is not founded on the testimony of God concerning His Son, if it is not founded upon what the Father testifies regarding the accepted offering of His beloved Son, is not a solid peace. Tell anxious souls to try praise, notwithstanding; only point out to them this aspect of the matter—tell them to praise the Lamb; tell them to praise Him because He offered Himself as the sacrifice: tell them to fix their eye upon His blood. For, you notice, in the very act of so doing they have forgotten self. Self forgotten, it is the Lamb that is remembered. Worthy is the Lamb! I am all unworthiness; worthy is the Lamb! They have received what they sought.

Praise at Christ's Return

I have to make a closing remark. There is a song in reserve for us; Christ is coming, and there is to be a song then, such as we have never yet sung—at least, I suppose very likely that is what is meant by "the song of the Lamb." The song of Moses we know something of, but it is at the Sea of Glass that we shall sing this song of the Lamb. Christ used to sing when He was on earth. We referred to His singing before He went out to the Mount of Olives; and it is said of His people that they too, shall have a song on that very day when Christ comes (Isa. 30:27, 29), a song as in the night, when a holy solemnity is kept. Now, what may we think regarding that song? If the Lord Jesus, at His First Coming, in the night in which He instituted the Lord's Supper, Himself gave thanks in the name of God's Church for after ages, did He not also sing that song for His people, for none could sing as He did? Would you have liked to have heard Him singing it in the upper room?

In the narrative given by Mark, of this story of Gethsemane (14:51), we are told of a young man who seems to have crept under the bushes, wishing to listen to what went on. Perhaps that young man heard some of Christ's strong crying and unutterable groanings. And I think many of us would like to have gone into that upper room, and to have heard Him sing that song, before He went to the Garden. We cannot, however. The time is past; but there is a song in reserve for us which Christ will lead. Yes! we believe that Christ will sing this song Himself. It is written in Psalm 22:22, 25, "In the midst of the congregation will I praise Thee," "My praise shall be of Thee in the great congregation." Oh, what will it be to hear Christ singing then, leading the song of praise, and inviting all His ransomed to join Him! Our voices are only now being tuned for that day when we shall join Him in "The Song of the Lamb"—a song which will be forever, and ever.